SPANISH FOR THE YOUNG

–Action Words!

William C. Harvey, M.S.

Illustrations: Dre Design

BARRON'S

Para Alexandre

© Copyright 2012 by Barron's Educational Series, Inc.

All inquiries should be addressed to:
Barron's Educational Series, Inc.
250 Wireless Boulevard
Hauppauge, New York 11788
www.barronseduc.com

ISBN: 978-1-4380-0014-5

Library of Congress Control Number: 2011942197

Printed in the United States of America

9 8 7 6 5 4 3 2 1

CONTENTS

ABOUT THE AUTHOR

William C. Harvey is a Spanish teacher. He has written many books, including *Spanish Every Day*. His books and classes are fun because he makes learning easy for everyone. He wrote this book because he wanted boys and girls to know how exciting it is to use ACTION WORDS in Spanish.

CHAPTER UNO

1

Hablamos español

(We speak Spanish)

¡Hola, amigos!
(Hi, friends)

This is **Señorita Amiga**. She speaks both SPANISH and English. You can find her on many pages in this book. She will give you secrets about SPANISH, so that you can learn it easily—and very fast! Why don't you write her name here before we get started?

_____

ABOUT THIS BOOK

The language you speak is called English. But many people in the world don't speak English. They speak other languages—like French, Chinese, or SPANISH! This book will teach you how to understand and speak SPANISH. If you learn a little SPANISH every day, soon you will know two languages instead of one!

This book also has a **VOCABULARY LIST** of SPANISH and English words. Whenever you forget how to say something, you can look it up in the **VOCABULARY LIST**, which is found at the back of the book.

Start now by looking up the word "friend."
Write the word here.

_____

(To check your answer, look at the upside down word below.)

ANSWER:
amigo or amiga

Good! Now, are you all set to learn more about the SPANISH language? Let's begin with the most important part of all . . .

THE SOUNDS OF SPANISH

These are the five most important sounds of SPANISH. Once you learn them, you will be able to understand, speak, and read SPANISH words correctly.

The letters look just like English, but in SPANISH they have a different sound. Go ahead and say each one aloud three times.

A (like "ah") The doctor tells the boy to say "ah."

E (like "eh") The man who cannot hear well says "eh."

I (like "ee") The girl who is scared says "ee."

O (like "oh") The lady who is surprised says "oh."

U (like "oo") At night the owl says "oo."

Here's what these sounds look like inside SPANISH words. Can you say each one correctly?

Fiesta (fee-EHS*-tah) (*say this part LOUDER)
Mucho (MOO-choh)
Grande (GRAHN-deh)

Now look up the meanings in the VOCABULARY LIST of the following words and write them down:

American _____

English _____

Hispanic _____

Let's learn some other sounds in SPANISH. Practice each word three times, speaking a little faster every time:

The letter **J** sounds like an "H," like in the word "<u>h</u>appy":

SPANISH	HOW TO SAY IT	ENGLISH
<u>j</u>irafa	(hee-RAH-fah)	giraffe

The letter **H** in SPANISH has no sound at all:

| <u>h</u>uevo | (oo-EH-voh) | egg |

The letter **Z** sounds just like an "S":

| <u>z</u>apato | (sah-PAH-toh) | shoe |

Did you check what the words mean in English? Do it! Some SPANISH sounds are a little harder to say. These letters look funny, so be careful when you read each word aloud:

The SPANISH letter **LL** sounds a lot like a "Y," like in the word "<u>y</u>es":

| caba<u>ll</u>o | (kah-BAH-yoh) | horse |

The SPANISH letter **Ñ** sounds like "NY" in the word "ca<u>ny</u>on":

| ni<u>ñ</u>o | (NEEN-yoh) | boy |

When together, the letters **QU** sound like a "K":

| cha<u>qu</u>eta | (chah-KEH-tah) | jacket |

RR is another letter in SPANISH that is very different from ENGLISH. To say it correctly, you must "roll your Rs," which sounds a lot like a car motor—RRRRRR!! Read this word:

| ca<u>rr</u>o | (KAH-rroh) | car |

Remember that people will understand you even if your words aren't perfect, so just do the best you can! Go ahead—write the SPANISH word next to each picture below:

1. _caballo_

2. _____

3. _____

4. _____

5. _____

6. _____

7. _____

ANSWERS:
caballo, zapato, carro, huevo, jirafa, chaqueta, niño

Now fill in the missing letters, and then read everything aloud:

h_e_o   ca_al_o   c_r_o   _ira_a
ni_o   cha_ _ et_   _ap_to

ANSWERS:

	zapato	chaqueta	niño
jirafa	carro	caballo	huevo

THE BIG SECRET!

By now you have learned that most letters in SPANISH have one sound and one sound only! That means that in a word like **maní** (peanut) the "**m**" has only the sound of "m," the "**a**" is only pronounced as "ah," and so are the "**n**" and "**i**" (ee). So you KNOW that **maní** is pronounced mah-NEE.

Yes, SPANISH is pronounced <u>exactly the way it is written</u>. You have to say every letter:

edificio (eh d ee f EE s ee oh)

<u>Say the second to the last part of the word</u> louder when it ends in **a**, **e**, **i**, **o**, **u**, **n**, or **s**. <u>Otherwise, say the last part of the word louder</u>.

By the way, some SPANISH words have a little slanted line over a letter, like this **á**. This tells us to <u>say that part of the word louder</u> than the other parts:

María	(mah-REE-ah)	Mary
José	(hoh-SEH)	Joe

SPANISH WORDS YOU ALREADY KNOW

These words are exactly the same in both languages. But look! They sound different when you say them in SPANISH:

ENGLISH	SPANISH	HOW TO SAY IT
doctor	**doctor**	dohk-TOHR
animal	**animal**	ah-nee-MAHL
color	**color**	koh-LOHR
radio	**radio**	RAH-dee-oh
hospital	**hospital**	ohs-pee-TAHL

And these are some SPANISH words that we added to OUR language. Read them aloud now!

rodeo	**Los Angeles**
banana	**Florida**
taco	**San Francisco**
chocolate	**Colorado**
tortilla	**Nevada**

Now, underline all the SPANISH words you can find in the story below:

José is a doctor at a hospital grande in Los Angeles. He loves to eat tacos with lots of salsa. My amigo in Florida sells chocolate bananas. He loves going to the rodeo when he goes to Colorado.

ANSWERS:

*José is a **doctor** at a **hospital grande** in **Los Angeles**. He loves to eat **tacos** with lots of **salsa**. My **amigo** in **Florida** sells **chocolate bananas**. He loves going to the **rodeo** when he goes to **Colorado**.*

Mis palabras favoritas
(My favorite words)

These are the words that most people learn first. Notice that from now on we are not going to provide the SPANISH pronunciation. Why? Because you have learned how to pronounce already!

SPANISH	ENGLISH	Write it in SPANISH here
español	Spanish	*español*
nada	nothing	_____
sí	yes	_____
libro	book	_____
gracias	thank you	_____
bueno	good	_____
adiós	good-bye	_____
agua	water	_____
casa	house	_____
familia	family	_____
niña	girl	_____
hola	hi	_____
hombre	man	_____
sombrero	hat	_____
niño	boy	_____
mucho	a lot	_____
grande	big	_____

Let's practice! Connect each word with a matching picture:

1. *agua*
2. *sombrero*
3. *tres*
4. *niña*
5. *hombre*
6. *casa*

ANSWERS:

water, hat, three, girl, man, house

¡Secreto!

The letter "**y**" (ee) is a WORD in SPANISH! It means "and." Use it to put your words together:

niños y niñas   boys and girls
dos y tres   two and three

¿Hablas español?
(Do you speak Spanish?)

Say these things today in SPANISH instead of English:

Hi!	**¡Hola!**
Good morning.	**Buenos días.**
Good afternoon.	**Buenas tardes.**
Good night.	**Buenas noches.**
Excuse me.	**Con permiso.**
What's your name?	**¿Cómo te llamas?**
My name is _____.	**Me llamo _____.**
Please.	**Por favor.**
Thanks a lot.	**Muchas gracias.**
You're welcome.	**De nada.**

How are you?	*¿Cómo estás?*
Very well, thanks.	*Muy bien, gracias.*
And you?	*¿Y tú?*
What's going on?	*¿Qué pasa?*
Not much.	*Sin novedad.*
Do you speak Spanish?	*¿Hablas español?*
Yes, a little.	*Sí, un poquito.*
Do you understand?	*¿Entiendes?*
I'm sorry.	*Lo siento.*
I don't understand.	*No entiendo.*
Ready?	*¿Listos?*
Let's go!	*¡Vamos!*
Good-bye!	*¡Adiós!*
See you later!	*¡Hasta luego!*

¡Secreto!

Whenever you write a sentence in SPANISH, add an upside down mark like this one: " ¿ " in front of a question, and " ¡ " in front of an exclamation.

¿Cómo estás?   ¡Bien!

Now, connect the words that go together best.
And when you're done, read all of your answers aloud!

¡Hasta luego!	*Me llamo Carlos.*
Muchas gracias.	*Muy bien.*
¿Cómo estás?	*Sin novedad.*
¿Qué pasa?	*¡Adiós!*
¿Hablas español?	*Sí, un poquito.*
¿Cómo te llamas?	*De nada.*

ANSWERS:

¡Hasta luego!—¡Adiós!
Muchas gracias.—De nada.
¿Cómo estás?—Muy bien.

¿Qué pasa?—Sin novedad.
¿Hablas español?—Sí, un poquito.
¿Cómo te llamas?—Me llamo José.

¡Secreto!

It's also fun to say, "Me, too!" in SPANISH:
¡Yo, también!

¿Cómo estás?	¡Bien!	¡Yo, también!
(How are you?)	(Fine!)	(Me, too!)

Palabras importantes
(Important words)

Everyone who learns SPANISH has to know these important words. They are the numbers and the colors. Practice writing them now!

Los números
(Numbers)

uno   <u>uno</u>

dos   _____

tres   _____

cuatro   _____

cinco   _____

seis   _____

siete   _____

ocho   _____

nueve   _____

diez   _____

Soon you'll know how to count *anything!*

11 *once* _____	12 *doce* _____
13 *trece* _____	14 *catorce* _____
15 *quince* _____	16 *dieciséis* _____
17 *diecisiete* _____	18 *dieciocho* _____
19 *diecinueve* _____	20 *veinte* _____

30 *treinta* _____	40 *cuarenta* _____
50 *cincuenta* _____	60 *sesenta* _____
70 *setenta* _____	80 *ochenta* _____
90 *noventa* _____	100 *cien* _____

To say all the numbers in between, put them together like this:
21 = *veinte y uno*. Can you say these numbers in SPANISH?
Just add the word *y*:

32   ***treinta y dos***
35   _____
69   _____
91   _____

ANSWERS:
treinta y cinco, sesenta y nueve, noventa y uno

Now, practice by counting. Can you draw two hats, four houses, and three books, and then write their names in SPANISH?

ANSWERS:
dos sombreros, cuatro casas y tres libros

11

Here's another way to use numbers in SPANISH:

first	**primero**	sixth	**sexto**
second	**segundo**	seventh	**séptimo**
third	**tercero**	eighth	**octavo**
fourth	**cuarto**	ninth	**noveno**
fifth	**quinto**	tenth	**décimo**

Los colores
(The colors)

Write the name of each color and say it aloud!

blue	*azul*	<u>azul</u>
black	*negro*	_____
yellow	*amarillo*	_____
brown	*café*	_____
purple	*morado*	_____
red	*rojo*	_____
green	*verde*	_____
white	*blanco*	_____
pink	*rosado*	_____
orange	*anaranjado*	_____

Use this question to practice the colors in SPANISH!

¿De qué color es?
(What color is it?)

Es . . . (It's . . .)

 snow

banana

coal

pumpkin

grass

sky

dirt

fire

plum

ANSWERS:

morado	plum	*anaranjado*	sky
rojo	fire	*negro*	pumpkin
café	dirt	*amarillo*	coal
verde	grass	*blanco*	banana
			snow

¡Feliz cumpleaños!
(Happy birthday!)

Now that you know some *números* in SPANISH, try out this question and answer it right away!

How old are you?   I'm . . .
¿Cuántos años tienes?   *Tengo . . .*

Write your age in SPANISH here: _____

¡Secreto!

Whenever you talk about people, these little words will be very helpful:

I   *Yo*

You guys   *Ustedes*

You   *Tú*
He   *Él*
She   *Ella*

They (boys)   *Ellos*

We   *Nosotros*

They (girls)   *Ellas*

13

Más práctica con los colores
(More practice with the colors)

SPANISH words are put together differently. To say what color something is, put the color <u>after</u> the word instead of before.

Color these pictures as you read the words!

the <u>green</u> car
el carro <u>verde</u>

the <u>brown</u> cow
la vaca <u>café</u>

The yellow ball
La pelota amarilla

The blue book
El libro azul

The black shoe
El zapato negro

¡Secreto!

Did you notice that in SPANISH the word **el** or **la** appears in front of words that name people and things? Most of the time, words that end with **o** have **el** in front . . .

el libro   el sombrero   el amigo

. . . whereas words that end in **a** have **la** in front:

la niña   la casa   la banana

And what do **el** and **la** mean? They mean "the"!

¡Mucha acción!
(Lots of action!)

The best SPANISH words are the ones that mean ACTION. These say what people do:

beber	drink
caminar	walk
dormir	sleep
escribir	write
correr	run
hablar	talk
jugar	play
leer	read
comer	eat

Sometimes ACTION WORDS change a little when you talk in SPANISH, but they are easy to learn!

ENGLISH	SPANISH	
I talk	Hablo	(AH-bloh)
I read	Leo	(LEH-oh)
I write	Escribo	(ehs-KREE-boh)

¡Secreto!

> In SPANISH, you don't have to say "I" (*Yo*) with your ACTION WORD if you don't want to:
> *Hablo* and *Yo hablo* mean the same thing!

Can you guess what all of these words mean?

Hablo, leo y escribo en español.

ANSWER:
I talk, I read, and I write in Spanish.

Buscapalabras 1
(Word Search 1)

And now, find these words inside the puzzle below.

WARNING: IT IS HARD! The words can be written left-to-right, right-to-left, up-down, down-up, and in diagonal! Let's see how good you are at this.

**AGUA • CASA • HOLA • CINCO • LIBRO • MUCHO • BUENO
PELOTA • SOMBRERO • FAMILIA • AMIGO • BLANCO**

```
O  C  N  I  C  C  T  J  J  M  L  Z  L  O  X
Z  Q  H  E  Z  N  F  W  S  A  A  I  C  F  X
A  Z  R  O  R  E  R  B  M  O  S  N  B  P  Q
H  I  P  Q  M  F  Q  G  X  L  A  R  E  R  Y
B  A  L  Y  N  T  B  A  M  L  U  T  F  B  O
U  U  D  I  O  J  X  T  B  X  U  D  H  V  X
E  G  O  E  M  A  B  O  H  O  F  M  B  K  A
N  A  L  U  M  A  G  L  Q  Q  V  T  P  L  Q
O  M  A  U  E  N  F  E  O  Y  G  J  O  I  E
I  Y  C  S  G  P  M  P  F  H  C  H  N  X  D
C  H  I  H  A  T  D  R  G  H  N  X  S  W  H
O  G  A  B  J  C  C  B  G  E  U  B  N  C  H
A  M  Q  L  K  V  M  N  T  P  B  M  X  A  F
A  M  I  G  O  G  K  N  B  Q  T  D  I  T  R
T  U  U  U  C  V  Q  G  Q  P  J  E  X  B  I
```

Find the answers on page 129.

2 CHAPTER
DOS

La mañana
(Morning)

Mi cuarto
(My room)

Learn SPANISH in your bedroom every morning! First, name everything around you:

bed	*la cama*
closet	*el ropero*
dresser	*el tocador*
door	*la puerta*
window	*la ventana*
alarm clock	*el despertador*
floor	*el piso*
pillow	*la almohada*
blanket	*la frazada*
sheet	*la sábana*
bedspread	*el cubrecama*
pajamas	*el pijama*
clothes	*la ropa*

Now, name four things that go ON a bed. Write in SPANISH!

la almohada

_____

_____

_____

ANSWERS:

la frazada
el cubrecama
la sábana

¡Secreto!

The word for bedroom in SPANISH is *el dormitorio*.
The word for room is *el cuarto*. You can say either one!

THE AMAZING WORD "ES"

The word **Es** means "It's" or "Is" in SPANISH:

It's the bed.
Es la cama.

It's the closet.
Es el ropero.

Try some more:

The bed is blue.   **La cama es azul.**
The closet is white. **El ropero es blanco.**

Your turn:

It's the dresser.   _____
The dresser is brown. _____

ANSWERS:
Es el tocador.
El tocador es café.

Did You Say "My" (**mi**)

or "Your" (**tu**)?

Sit on your bed and practice saying "my" and "your" in SPANISH:

It's <u>my</u> pillow.   **Es <u>mi</u> almohada.**
It's <u>your</u> blanket. **Es <u>tu</u> frazada.**

It's <u>my</u> sheet.   **Es <u>mi</u> sábana.**
It's <u>your</u> bedspread. **Es <u>tu</u> cubrecama.**

Unscramble the SPANISH words in each phrase below, write the correct sentence on the right, and then SAY WHAT IT MEANS!

cuarto mi Es _____

tu Es ventana _____

despertador Es tu _____

mi Es ropero _____

puerta Es mi _____

ANSWERS:

AND WHAT IS *LOS* AND *LAS*?

To talk about more than one person or thing in SPANISH, change the *el* to *los*:

the boy
el niño

the boys
los niños

the big boys
los niños grandes*

And change the *la* to *las*:

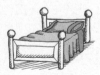

the bed
la cama

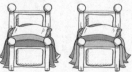

the beds
las camas

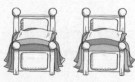

the white beds
las camas blancas*

*You need to add *s* to the describing word, too.

20

Acción para todos los días
(Action for every day)

Learn to talk about what <u>you do</u> every day. What do <u>you do</u> first in the morning?

Every day . . .   *Todos los días . . .*

I <u>turn off</u> the alarm clock.
   Apago *el despertador.*

I <u>get out of</u> the bed.
   Bajo *de la cama.*

I <u>walk</u> toward the closet.
   Camino *hacia el ropero.*

I <u>put away</u> the pajamas.
   Guardo *el piyama.*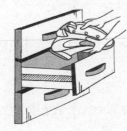

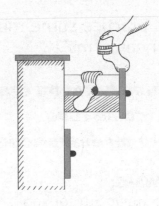

I <u>look for</u> the clothes.
   Busco *la ropa.*

Look closely! What is the last letter in all these words? _____

Apago   Guardo   Bajo   Camino   Busco

¡Secreto!

All these words end in **o** because they talk about <u>what I do</u> every day!

Ubicación
(Location)

Try out these new words today! Read the sentences aloud and then translate them.

toward = **hacia**
Camino <u>hacia</u> el ropero. _____

from = **de**
Camino <u>de</u> mi cuarto. _____

to = **a**
Camino <u>a</u> la puerta. _____

through = **por**
Camino <u>por</u> la casa. _____

ANSWERS:

I walk toward the closet. I walk from my room.
I walk to the door. I walk through the house.

Let's practice some more. Fill in the lines below. Remember that the word *mi* means "my"!

Camino hacia mi cama. <u>I walk toward my bed.</u>
Guardo mi ropa. _____
Busco mi despertador. _____

ANSWERS:

I put away my clothes. I look for my alarm clock.

Did you fill in all the lines correctly? *¡Muy bien!*

Más acción
(More action)

Here are more things you do in the morning:

 I listen. *Escucho.*

 I yawn. *Bostezo.*

 I speak. *Hablo.*

I listen to the alarm clock.   *Escucho el despertador.*
I yawn a lot.   *Bostezo mucho.*
I speak SPANISH!   *¡Hablo español!*

Look! This is a story in SPANISH that you can understand:

*Todos los días apago mi despertador, bostezo y bajo de la cama.
Camino hacia el tocador, guardo mi piyama y busco la ropa en
el ropero. Hablo español en mi casa todos los días.*

ANSWERS:

Every day I turn off my alarm, I yawn, and I get out of bed. I walk
toward the dresser, put away my pajamas, and I look for clothes
in the closet. I speak Spanish in my house every day.

¡Secreto!

This is something you need to learn right away:
¡Que tenga buen día!   Have a nice day!

Let's stop for a minute. Unscramble these letters and practice each
SPANISH action word:

agorud _____   *ccsoheu* _____
ebzoost _____   *moanic* _____
cbsou _____

ANSWERS:
camino   escucho   busco   bostezo   guardo

Más cosas
(More things)

Do you want to know more SPANISH? Let's name other things in the bedroom:

bookshelf	*el librero*	
lamp	*la lámpara*	
clock	*el reloj*	
table	*la mesa*	
chair	*la silla*	
computer	*la computadora*	

And don't forget your favorite words!

Los juguetes
(Toys)

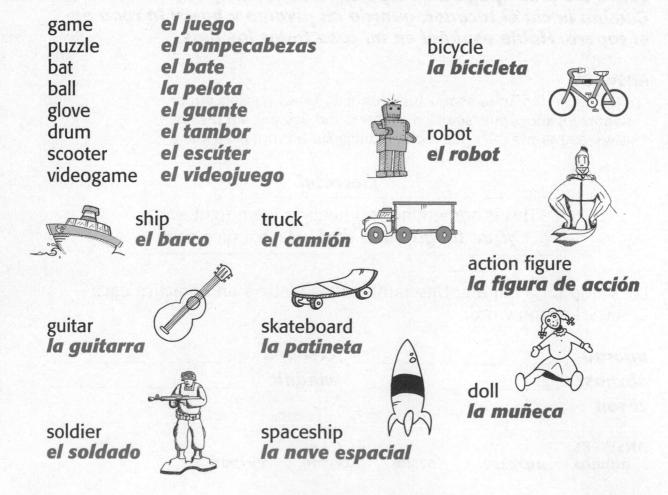

game	*el juego*
puzzle	*el rompecabezas*
bat	*el bate*
ball	*la pelota*
glove	*el guante*
drum	*el tambor*
scooter	*el escúter*
videogame	*el videojuego*

bicycle
la bicicleta

robot
el robot

ship
el barco

truck
el camión

action figure
la figura de acción

guitar
la guitarra

skateboard
la patineta

doll
la muñeca

soldier
el soldado

spaceship
la nave espacial

Try out these new actions:

> I look at (or watch) the . . . **_Miro . . ._**
> I point to the . . . **_Señalo . . ._**

I look at the computer. **_Miro la computadora._**
I point to the toy. **_Señalo el juguete._**

Make a sentence! Fill in all the correct words below:

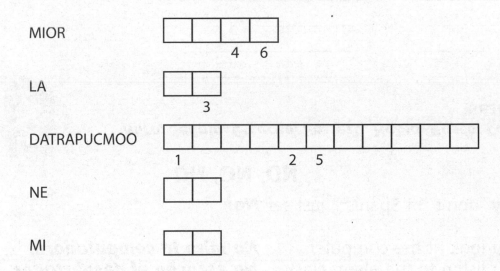

MIOR   □ □ □ □
           4 6

LA   □ □
       3

DATRAPUCMOO   □ □ □ □ □ □ □ □ □ □ □
              1   2 5

NE   □ □

MI   □ □

Now, look at the numbers above, and fill in the last word.

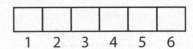

□ □ □ □ □ □
1 2 3 4 5 6

ANSWERS:
MIRO LA COMPUTADORA EN MI CUARTO

¡Secreto!

> Put all your SPANISH together!
>
> I look at the <u>white</u> computer.
> **_Miro la computadora <u>blanca</u>._**
>
> I point to the <u>black</u> bike.
> **_Señalo la bicicleta <u>negra</u>._**

25

Write a list of all the ACTIONS you have learned so far. There are ten!

Apago	I turn off
Guardo	I put away
Bajo	_____
_____	_____
_____	_____
_____	_____
_____	_____
_____	_____
_____	_____

ANSWERS:

Miro, Señalo, Escucho, Bostezo, Hablo, Busco, Camino

NO, NO, NO

To say "don't" in Spanish, just say *No!*

I don't look at the computer.	***No miro la computadora.***
I don't listen to the alarm clock.	***No escucho el despertador.***
I don't put away my toys.	***No guardo mis juguetes.***

You try:

I don't put away my pajamas.	_____
I don't get out of bed.	_____

ANSWERS:

No guardo mi piyama. No bajo de la cama.

Some SPANISH ACTION WORDS are very special, so you should spend extra time learning them:

I wake up.	***Me despierto.***
I take a bath.	***Me baño.***
I comb my hair.	***Me peino.***
I take off.	***Me quito.***
I put on.	***Me pongo.***

   Todos los días me despierto, me baño, me peino, me quito el piyama y me pongo la ropa.

¿Qué hora es?
(What time is it?)

We don't want to be late, so let's tell time in SPANISH. You may need to see the numbers on pages 10 and 11 for this. First say the hour . . .

It's six o'clock.
***Son las* seis.**

It's eight o'clock.
***Son las* ocho.**

. . . and then add the minutes:

It's 6:10.
***Son las* seis y diez.**

It's 8:45.
***Son las* ocho y cuarenta y cinco.**

Okay. Place the correct time next to each clock. The first one is done for you:

Es la una y treinta.

_____

_____

_____

_____

ANSWERS:

7:45	*Son las siete y cuarenta y cinco.*
12:00	*Son las doce.*
3:20	*Son las tres y veinte.*
4:15	*Son las cuatro y quince.*

27

This is how you say "at" a certain time:

At 6:00   *A las seis*
At 8:20   *A las ocho y veinte*
At 5:05   *A las cinco y cinco*

Read these aloud:

I turn off the alarm at 7:00.
Apago el despertador a las siete.

I get out of bed at 7:10.
Bajo de la cama a las siete y diez.

¡Secreto!

Remember you can practice saying the time anytime you see a clock! Try telling the time in SPANISH right now!

La ropa
(Clothing)

You put on clothing every day. Use this new ACTION WORD as you talk about what you wear:

Uso . . .
I wear . . .

t-shirt
la camiseta

shirt
la camisa

dress
el vestido

shoes
los zapatos

pants
los pantalones

skirt
la falda

I <u>also</u> wear . . .
También uso . . .

shorts	sweater	socks
los pantalones cortos	*el suéter*	*los calcetines*

belt	jacket	cap
el cinturón	*la chaqueta*	*la gorra*

Practice reading aloud:

Uso la camiseta y los pantalones.
Uso los calcetines y los zapatos.
Uso la falda y el cinturón.

You already know these ACTION WORDS. Say them every morning with your clothing:

I look for . . .   *Busco . . .*
                              Busco mi chaqueta.
I put away . . .   *Guardo . . .*
                              Guardo mi camisa.

This is easy. Try practicing this question with a friend:

What do you do in the morning?
¿Qué haces por la mañana?

¡Secreto!

Watch your SPANISH grow!

¿Qué haces?
What do you do?
      ¿Qué haces por la mañana?
      What do you do in the morning?
            ¿Qué haces por la mañana todos los días?
            What do you do in the morning every day?

Una conversación
(A conversation)

Grab a friend and practice this conversation:

Hi, Carlitos. What do you do in the morning?
Hola, Carlitos. ¿Qué haces por la mañana?

    Me? I wake up, take off my pajamas,
    and put on my clothes. And you, Rosita?

    ¿Yo? Me despierto, me quito el piyama
    y me pongo la ropa. ¿Y tú, Rosita?

Me? I turn off the alarm at seven, but I don't get out of bed!
¿Yo? Apago el despertador a las siete, ¡pero no bajo
de la cama!

WHAT IS *UN* AND *UNA*?

This is how you say "a" or "an" in SPANISH. Use *un* with words that end in *o*:

    A boy   *Un niño*

    A shoe   *Un zapato*

And *una* with words that end in *a*:

    A ball   *Una pelota*

    A skirt   *Una falda*

Read these SPANISH words aloud:

I turn off an alarm clock.	*Apago un despertador.*
I wear a sweater.	*Uso un suéter.*
I look at a computer.	*Miro una computadora.*

Let's practice what we've learned. Draw lines from the SPANISH sentences to the correct English sentences and read aloud:

Busco la pelota.	I wake up at six.
No bajo de la cama.	I wear a black jacket.
Apago el despertador.	What color is it?
Me despierto a las seis.	I look for the ball.
Hablo poquito español.	What do you do?
Miro el juguete grande.	I put away the clothes.
Guardo la ropa.	I look at the big toy.
¿Qué haces?	I speak a little Spanish.
Uso una chaqueta negra.	I turn off the alarm clock.
¿De qué color es?	I don't get out of bed.

Did you understand everything? Check your answers!

ANSWERS:

¿De qué color es? — What color is it?
Uso una chaqueta negra. — I wear a black jacket.
¿Qué haces? — What do you do?
Guardo la ropa. — I put away the clothes.
Miro el juguete grande. — I look at the big toy.
Hablo poquito español. — I speak a little Spanish.
Me despierto a las seis. — I wake up at six.
Apago el despertador. — I turn off the alarm clock.
No bajo de la cama. — I don't get out of bed.
Busco la pelota. — I look for the ball.

Buscapalabras 2
(Word Search 2)

Okay, find these words inside the puzzle below.

Remember that the words can be side-to-side, up-and-down, and every other way!

APAGO • USO • MIRO • HABLO • GUARDO
BAJO • BOSTEZO • BUSCO • CAMINO • ESCUCHO

```
O  O  S  U  Y  O  N  P  B  W  M  R
P  U  X  I  C  S  E  R  Z  F  I  X
W  M  V  S  A  S  T  Y  A  V  R  K
E  A  U  B  C  O  Z  E  T  S  O  B
O  B  P  U  W  Z  K  S  E  R  D  X
T  N  C  A  Q  T  R  S  B  W  R  O
T  H  I  F  G  R  I  Y  J  B  A  R
O  L  O  M  R  O  E  Q  A  B  U  J
V  X  U  P  A  Z  A  J  H  D  G  P
H  A  B  L  O  C  O  R  T  S  M  Q
Q  C  H  K  U  G  K  V  M  N  P  H
Z  N  F  S  F  X  K  K  O  M  S  N
```

The answers are on page 129.

Believe me, SPANISH gets easier and easier when you take the time to practice. Now, let's leave the bedroom and learn more ACTION WORDS!

3 CHAPTER
TRES

Por toda la casa
(All through the house)

Speaking SPANISH around the house is easy! That's because many SPANISH words are a lot like English. Let's see if you can guess what all these words mean:

el apartamento _____

el condominio _____

la mansión _____

la chimenea _____

el balcón _____

el estéreo _____

el refrigerador _____

el sofá _____

la televisión _____

el acondicionador de aire _____

la electricidad _____

la planta artificial _____

ANSWERS:

apartment, condominium, mansion chimney, balcony, stereo, refrigerator, sofa, television air conditioner, electricity, artificial plant

Now add ACTION WORDS to the words above:

Apago _____ (stereo)

Camino hacia _____ (sofa)

Miro _____ (television)

Bajo _____ (balcony)

Busco _____ (apartment)

ANSWERS:

Apago el estéreo.
Camino hacia el sofá.
Miro la televisión.
Bajo al* balcón.
Busco el apartamento.
(*In this case, "to the" is *al*)

La familia
(The family)

Do you see any of these people around the house? Say *Buenos días* to your family every morning.

mother
la madre
wife
la esposa

father
el padre
husband
el marido

daughter
la hija
sister
la hermana

son
el hijo
brother
el hermano

grandmother
la abuela

grandfather
el abuelo

aunt
la tía

uncle
el tío

cousins
las primas

cousins
los primos

parents
los padres

relatives
los parientes

All families are different. Fill in the blanks with the first names of people in your *familia*:

_____ *es mi hermana.*	_____ is my sister.
_____ *es mi padre.*	_____ is my father.
_____ *es mi tía.*	_____ is my aunt.
_____ *es mi hermano.*	_____ is my brother.
_____ *es mi madre.*	_____ is my mother.
_____ *es mi abuelo.*	_____ is my grandpa.

Ask someone in your *familia* to practice SPANISH with you. Then read #1 while the other person reads #2:

#1:   *Hola,* (the person's name).
#2:   *Buenos días,* (your name).
#1:   *¿Cómo estás?*
#2:   *Bien, ¿y tú?*
#1:   *Muy bien, gracias.*

THE LITTLE WORD *SU*

To say "his" or "her" in SPANISH, use the little word, *su*:

Linda es su hermana.   Linda is his sister.
Victor es su padre.   Victor is her father.

Fill in the blanks!

It's her uncle.	*Es su* _____.
It's his room.	*Es* _____ *cuarto.*
It's her toy.	*Es su* _____.
It's his jacket.	*Es* _____.
It's her computer.	_____.

ANSWERS:

tío
su
juguete
su chaqueta
Es su computadora.

Underline every other letter to find out the secret message. The first letter is done for you:

A̲sousftabmuirlminaenxozelsomduaylgorsatnadre.

ANSWER:

Su familia no es muy grande.

¡Secreto!

The word "people" is *la gente* in SPANISH and the word "person" is *la persona*.

Busco la persona.	I look for the person.
Busco la gente.	I look for the people.

Acción en la casa
(Action in the house)

We learned in Chapter **Dos** that ACTION WORDS tell what we do every day:

Apago.   I turn off.
Apago el despertador.

Camino.   I walk.
Camino en la casa.

Guardo.   I put away.
Guardo mi ropa.

Now let's learn some more. These words also end with the letter **o** because they say what I do:

Every day . . .	*Todos los días . . .*
I turn on the lamp.	*prendo la lámpara.*
I open the door.	*abro la puerta.*
I drink water.	*bebo agua.*
I read and I write.	*leo y escribo.*
I learn more SPANISH.	*aprendo más español.*

Take a minute to write these words in SPANISH:

I write _____ I drink _____ I learn _____
I read _____ I open _____ I turn on _____

This time write in English:

Escribo en el libro.   _____

No abro las ventanas.   _____

Prendo la computadora.   _____

ANSWERS:

I write in the book.
I don't open the windows.
I turn on the computer.

Did you fill in all the lines correctly? *¡Muy bien!*
Now try these other ACTION WORDS in SPANISH:

I live.	*Vivo.*	*Vivo en California.*
I eat.	*Como.*	*Como mucho chocolate.*
I run.	*Corro.*	*No corro en la casa.*

Connect the words with opposite meanings.

Camino	*Hablo*
Uso	*Apago*
Leo	*Guardo*
Prendo	*Escribo*
Escucho	*Corro*

ANSWERS:

Hablo	*Escucho*
Apago	*Prendo*
Escribo	*Leo*
Guardo	*Uso*
Corro	*Camino*

¿Cómo es?
(What does he or she look like?)

Say these words as you move around the house. Point to each person that you see:

Es . . . He is . . . or She is . . .

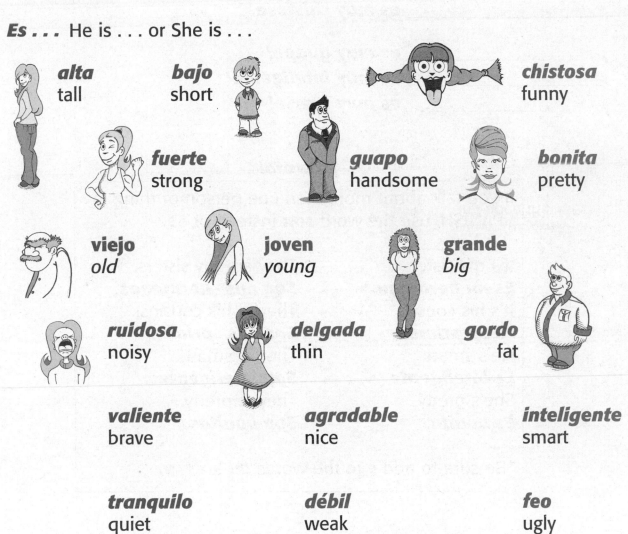

alta
tall

bajo
short

chistosa
funny

fuerte
strong

guapo
handsome

bonita
pretty

viejo
old

joven
young

grande
big

ruidosa
noisy

delgada
thin

gordo
fat

valiente
brave

agradable
nice

inteligente
smart

tranquilo
quiet

débil
weak

feo
ugly

Don't forget to change the final **o** to **a** when you talk about girls or women, and **a** to **o** when you talk about boys or men! What do these words mean in English?

> **Mi padre es baj_o_, guap_o_ y chistos_o_,
> y mi madre es alt_a_, delgad_a_ y bonit_a_.**

ANSWERS:

My father is short, handsome, and funny, and my mother is tall, thin, and pretty.

39

Put different names next to the words below. Think of famous people, friends, or even someone who lives in your house!

¡_____ es muy bonita!

¡_____ es muy valiente!

¡_____ es muy chistosa!

¡_____ es muy guapo!

¡_____ es muy inteligente!

¡_____ es muy fuerte!

¡Secreto!

If you talk about more than one person or thing in SPANISH, use the word **son** <u>instead</u> of **es**:

It's my sister.		They are my sisters.
Es mi hermana.	→	*Son mis* hermanas.*
It's his cousin.		They're his cousins.
Es su primo.	→	*Son sus* primos.*
He's smart.		They're smart.
Es inteligente.	→	*Son inteligentes.*
She's pretty.		They're pretty.
Es bonita.	→	*Son bonitas.*

*Be sure to add **s** to the words **mi** and **su**.

Las cosas en la casa
(Things in the house)

You talked in SPANISH about the family. Now it's time to name parts of the house:

I walk toward the . . .
Camino hacia . . .

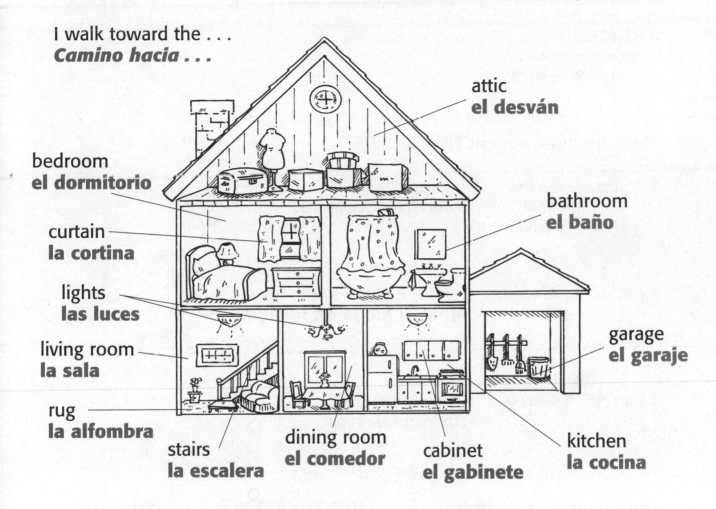

attic
el desván

bedroom
el dormitorio

bathroom
el baño

curtain
la cortina

lights
las luces

living room
la sala

garage
el garaje

rug
la alfombra

stairs
la escalera

dining room
el comedor

cabinet
el gabinete

kitchen
la cocina

Cross out the one word that doesn't belong with the others:

la ventana, la hermana, las cortinas
el carro, el garaje, el soldado
el juguete, la cocina, el comedor
la lámpara, las luces, la falda
el libro, el piso, el techo

ANSWERS:

la hermana
el soldado
el juguete
la falda
el libro

41

Add your ACTION WORDS! Write in SPANISH:

I eat in the kitchen.   *Como en la cocina.*
I open the curtain.   _____
I turn on the lights.   _____

Here are three new ACTION WORDS:

I go up.   *Subo.*   I go up the stairs.
                         Subo las escaleras.

I put in.   *Meto.*   I put the game in the box.
                         Meto el juego en la caja.

I sweep.   *Barro.*   I sweep the attic.
                         Barro el desván.

Put these letters in order to make ACTION WORDS in SPANISH:

bous _____   *rabor* _____   *otme* _____

¿Dónde está?
(Where is it? Where is he? Where is she?)

Use the word *está* to tell where something or someone is.

The rug is in the bedroom.
La alfombra está en el dormitorio.

My father is in his room.
Mi padre está en su cuarto.

Fill in the word *está* and write what the words mean in English:

Tony está en el comedor.   Tony is in the dining room.

Mi hermana ____ en el garaje.   _____

El baño ____ en la casa.   _____

La muñeca ____ en el piso.   _____

Tu camisa ____ en la sala.   _____

ANSWERS:

Your shirt is in the living room.
The doll is on the floor.
The bathroom is in the house.
My sister is in the garage.

¡Secreto!

> Use *están* when you are talking about more than one person or thing:
>
> Where <u>are they</u>?   <u>They're</u> in the kitchen.
> *¿Dónde están?*   *Están en la cocina.*
>
> <u>They are</u> in the bathroom.
> *Están en el baño.*

Más cosas en la casa
(More things in the house)

Move from room to room, learning the names for everything in SPANISH.

I look for the . . .   *Busco* . . .

el sofá
couch

el refrigerador
refrigerator

la estufa
stove

la lavadora
washer

la secadora
dryer

el bote de basura
trashcan

el sillón
armchair

el escritorio
desk

el televisor
television

Look what you can say!

The couch is in the living room.
El sofa está en la sala.

The trashcans are in the garage.
Los botes de basura están en el garaje.

The television is not in the bedroom.
El televisor no está en el dormitorio.

Your turn:

The stove is in the kitchen. _____.

ANSWER:

La estufa está en la cocina.

Write the names of furniture in SPANISH on little sticky notes. Then, stick them on everything so you won't forget!

Now—let's put these things into ACTION. What do these words mean?

Leo en el sillón.	<u>I read in the armchair.</u>
Escribo en el escritorio.	_____
Prendo el televisor.	_____
Meto la ropa en la lavadora.	_____
Abro el refrigerador.	_____

Now unscramble the letters *and then* write what the words mean in English:

	ESPAÑOL	ENGLISH
la raavload	_____	_____
el veroteils	_____	_____
la fuetas	_____	_____

ANSWERS:

la estufa	stove
el televisor	television
la lavadora	washer

I open the refrigerator.
I put clothes in the washer.
I turn on the television.
I write at the desk.

¡Secreto!

There are two ways to say "they" in SPANISH:

Ellos and **Ellas**

They are friends. (boys)   ***Ell<u>os</u> son amig<u>os</u>.***
They are friends. (girls)   ***Ell<u>as</u> son amig<u>as</u>.***

¿Dónde?
(Where?)

These next SPANISH words will help you find what you're looking for. Start with the word **en**, which can mean "in," "at," or "on":

Como en la cocina, en la mesa y en la silla.
I eat <u>in</u> the kitchen, <u>at</u> the table, and <u>on</u> the chair.

Do you want to know where everybody and everything is? Look at these people:

Finish these sentences with any of the words above:

He's outside.	***Está***	_____.
She's inside.	***Está***	_____.
They're there.	***Están***	_____.
I look behind.	***Busco***	_____.
I look under.	***Miro***	_____.

ANSWERS:

afuera   adentro   allí   detrás   debajo

Describo
(I Describe)

Use these words to describe the things in your *casa*:

viejo	***nuevo***		***limpio***	***sucio***
old	new		clean	dirty

frío	***caliente***	***lleno***	***vacío***	***caro***	***barato***
cold	hot	full	empty	expensive	cheap

Practice describing everything you see:

El sillón es nuevo.	The armchair is new.
Las cortinas están limpias.	The curtains are clean.
La estufa está caliente.	The stove is hot.

Bien. Now finish these with the missing word:

It's dirty.   ***Está*** _____.

It's full.   ***Está*** _____.

It's cold.   ***Está*** _____.

ANSWERS:

frío   lleno   sucio

¡Secreto!

When you talk about a thing that ends in **o**, the word that describes it usually does, too:

El teléfono es negro y bonito. The phone is black and pretty.

And, if the name of the thing ends in **a**, then what we say about it often ends in **a**:

La silla negra es bonita. The black chair is pretty.

47

Now, connect the words that mean the opposite:

enfrente	*caro*
arriba	*lejos*
frío	*ella*
afuera	*allí*
él	*adentro*
cerca	*caliente*
barato	*detrás*
aquí	*abajo*

ANSWERS:

allí	*aquí*
caro	*barato*
lejos	*cerca*
ella	*él*
adentro	*afuera*
caliente	*frío*
abajo	*arriba*
detrás	*enfrente*

Keep speaking SPANISH around the house. Can you figure out what's going on here?

Vivo en un apartamento con mi padre, mi madre y mi hermana. Siempre subo las escaleras y corro hacia el cuarto de mi madre. Abro la puerta y prendo su computadora. Meto el CD, leo y escribo, y aprendo mucho español.

ANSWERS:

I live in an apartment with my father, my mom and my sister. I always go up the stairs and run toward my mother's room. I open the door and I turn on her computer. I put in the CD, I read and I write, and I learn a lot of Spanish.

48

¡Secreto!

These are great questions about you and your *casa*:

Where do you live?   I live in _____.
¿Dónde vives?   *Vivo en _____.*

What's your address?   My address is _____.
¿Cuál es tu dirección?   *Mi dirección es _____.*

What's your phone number?   My number is _____.
¿Cuál es tu número de teléfono?   *Mi número es _____.*

¿Cuándo?
(When?)

Add one of these words to
tell <u>when</u> you do something:

hoy   today
mañana   tomorrow
ayer   yesterday

Try a few more:

always   *siempre*
I always speak SPANISH.   *<u>Siempre</u> hablo español.*

never   *nunca*
I never run in the house.   *<u>Nunca</u> corro en la casa.*

sometimes   *a veces*
I sometimes eat chocolate.   *<u>A veces</u> como chocolate.*

So, *cuándo* do you practice your *español*?

_____

Buscapalabras 3
(Word Search 3)

Find these words inside the puzzle below!

ABRO • APRENDO • BEBO • COMO • CORRO
ESCRIBO • LEO • PRENDO • SUBO • VIVO

```
E  T  B  O  A  N  G  A  T  U  V  K  W  N  V
N  S  B  G  Q  U  W  T  V  Q  J  I  E  U  G
H  E  C  K  E  S  E  J  U  W  F  B  V  S  G
B  R  E  R  I  B  S  R  V  O  M  Y  Q  O  O
F  S  S  K  I  V  T  C  V  T  M  Z  O  U  V
Q  R  O  Q  O  B  A  K  X  Y  F  L  N  R  U
N  G  S  D  L  R  O  E  G  Y  C  E  X  E  Y
Y  F  C  Z  P  H  B  E  F  Y  O  O  K  J  D
R  S  C  G  U  I  V  A  P  L  B  Q  A  G  R
I  V  L  W  T  X  L  Q  N  P  U  N  P  X  K
T  M  J  K  Z  G  D  A  R  N  S  U  R  F  A
G  Q  S  M  J  H  C  E  O  O  Q  K  E  V  L
O  R  R  O  C  Z  N  C  O  M  O  Q  N  S  E
X  S  C  I  U  D  J  K  Z  I  K  R  D  H  H
G  D  X  Q  O  V  V  A  Y  H  P  L  O  U  P
```

The answers are on page 129.

We're not finished yet! Let's go to another part of the house to learn more ACTION WORDS . . .

4 CHAPTER
CUATRO

A la cocina
(To the kitchen)

¿Cómo estás?
(How are you?)

On your way to the kitchen, find out how everyone is feeling today:

I am . . .   *Estoy . . .*

fine *bien*

happy *feliz*

sad *triste*

	BOYS	**GIRLS**
excited	*emocionado*	*emocionada*
tired	*cansado*	*cansada*
angry	*enojado*	*enojada*

So, how are you today? Put in the words you like:

Are you . . .?   *¿Estás* _____*?*
No. I am . . .   *No. Estoy* _____*.*

Use the words *estoy* and *estás* to talk about how you feel and where you are.

Where are you?	*¿Dónde estás?*
I'm in the kitchen.	*Estoy en la cocina.*
How are you?	*¿Cómo estás?*
I'm fine.	*Estoy bien.*

¡Secreto!

The word **muy** means "very" and the word **mucho** means "a lot":

I'm very tired.	*Estoy <u>muy</u> cansado.*
I walk to school a lot.	*Camino <u>mucho</u> a la escuela.*

Tengo hambre
(I'm hungry)

The word **Tengo** is very important in SPANISH. Read each sentence aloud:

I'm hungry.	**Tengo hambre.**
I'm thirsty.	**Tengo sed.**
I'm scared.	**Tengo miedo.**
I'm ten years old.	**Tengo diez años.**
I have many friends.	**Tengo muchos amigos.**

Connect these words with the pictures below:

Tengo miedo.   **Tengo dos amigos.**   **Tengo sed.**

Does speaking SPANISH make you hungry? Go into the kitchen and find something to eat:

El desayuno
(Breakfast)

egg
el huevo

cheese
el queso

fruit
la fruta

meat
la carne

juice
el jugo

milk
la leche

bread
el pan

butter
la mantequilla

sandwich
el sandwich

toast
la tostada

tea
el té

jelly
la jalea

Here's another fun expression:

I like . . .   *Me gusta . . .*

Now talk about your favorite breakfast foods. Just fill in the blanks:

I like toast.   *Me gusta* <u>*el pan tostado*</u>.
I like cheese.   *Me gusta* _____.
I like _____.   *Me gusta el jugo.*

ANSWERS:
juice
el queso

¡Secreto!

These foods are the same as English!

cereal	*el cereal*
waffles	*los waffles*
yogurt	*el yogurt*

La acción de ayer
(Yesterday's action)

Before we learn any more ACTION WORDS,
practice some that you already know:

Comí

camino	I walk	*escribo*	I write
uso	I wear	*subo*	I climb
bajo	I get down	*aprendo*	I learn
hablo	I speak	*como*	I eat
guardo	I put away	*bebo*	I drink
miro	I look at	*corro*	I run
escucho	I listen	*abro*	I open

These words end in **o** because they talk about <u>WHAT I DO</u> every day. To talk about <u>WHAT I DID</u> already, we need to change the last letter to either **é** or **í**.

Escribí

caminé	I walked	*escribí*	I wrote
usé	I wore	*subí*	I climbed
bajé	I got down	*aprendí*	I learned
hablé	I spoke	*comí*	I ate
guardé	I put away	*bebí*	I drank
miré	I looked at	*corrí*	I ran
escuché	I listened	*abrí*	I opened

Practice! Write the little ´ (accent mark) on top of the **e** and **i**:

e   e   e   e   i   i   i   i   i

After you put the accent mark on the last letter, write each of these words on the lines below:

comi   escuche   mire   abri

I ate _____

I listened _____

I looked at _____

I opened _____

Now you can say <u>what you do every day</u> AND <u>what you did yesterday</u>:

I speak SPANISH.   ***Hablo español.***
I spoke SPANISH yesterday.   ***Hablé español ayer.***

I drink milk.   ***Bebo leche.***
I drank milk yesterday.   ***Bebí leche ayer.***

Let's practice what we learned at breakfast. Fill in all the missing letters and complete the sentence:

p _a_ n   *Comí el __pan__.* (I ate the bread.)

_ ues _   *Comí el* _____. (_____)

_ ar _ e   *Comí la* _____. (_____)

h _ _ vo   *Comí el* _____. (_____)

_ r _ t _   *Comí la* _____. (_____)

ANSWERS:
fruta
huevo
carne
queso

El almuerzo
(Lunch)

This time, say these important words that tell everyone what you want next:

I want the . . .   *Quiero . . .*

salad   soup   hot dog
la ensalada   *la sopa*   *el perro caliente*

hamburger   french fries   dessert
la hamburguesa   *las papas fritas*   *el postre*

La cena
(Dinner)

chicken
el pollo

ham
el jamón

turkey
el pavo

fish
el pescado

steak
el bistec

vegetables
los vegetales

To practice, cross out the one word that doesn't belong with the other two:

leche, jugo, jamón
piso, pavo, pollo
pescado, desayuno, almuerzo
como, bebo, amigo

ANSWERS:
amigo
pescado
piso
jamón

It's time to learn more ACTION WORDS.
These are great for the kitchen:

I prepare	*Preparo*	I cook	*Cocino*
I prepared	*Preparé*	I cooked	*Cociné*
I wash	*Lavo*	I mix	*Mezclo*
I washed	*Lavé*	I mixed	*Mezclé*

57

Fill in the missing letters to say what you did <u>yesterday</u>:

Cocin__   la   carn__.
Mezcl__   los   v__g__tal__s.
Prepar__   __l   almu__rzo.

ANSWERS:

Preparé el almuerzo.
Mezclé los vegetales.
Cociné la carne.

¡Secreto!

The word "recipe" is **la receta** in SPANISH.
Do you know any good ones?

¿Dónde está <u>la receta</u>?

Las frutas y los vegetales
(Fruits and vegetables)

Look for fruits and vegetables in the kitchen. Then, touch each one as you practice aloud:

Also I want . . .   También quiero . . .

strawberry
la fresa

banana
el plátano

apple
la manzana

grape
la uva

watermelon
la sandía

orange
la naranja

Test yourself! Count all the fruit in SPANISH.

dos naranjas

_____

_____

_____

_____

ANSWERS:

doce plátanos
dos manzanas
tres fresas
una sandía

I ate . . .   _Comí . . ._

onion
la cebolla

potato
la papa

tomato
el tomate

lettuce
la lechuga

corn
el maíz

carrot
la zanahoria

celery
el apio

beans
los frijoles

cucumber
el pepino

What color matches with each vegetable?

amarillo   *la lechuga*
rojo   *la zanahoria*
anaranjado   *el tomate*
verde   *el maíz*

ANSWERS:

Now talk about what you did with all the fruits and vegetables:

I put away the lettuce.   *Guardé la lechuga.*
I looked at the grapes.   *Miré las uvas.*
I ate the celery.   *Comí el apio.*

Look what I did in my kitchen yesterday!

Preparé una ensalada grande en la cocina ayer.
I prepared a big salad in the kitchen yesterday.

And now, write these sentences in English and then put them in order, so they make sense when you read them together:

Mezclé los vegetales.   _____

Caminé hacia la cocina.   _____

Lavé los tomates y la lechuga.   _____

Comí la ensalada.   _____

Abrí el refrigerador.   _____

ANSWERS:

I ate the salad.
I mixed the vegetables.
I washed the tomatoes and the lettuce.
I opened the refrigerator.
I walked toward the kitchen.

It's time to try these other ACTION WORDS in the kitchen:

I weigh	*Peso*	I freeze	*Congelo*
I weighed	*Pesé*	I froze	*Congelé*

I share	*Comparto*
I shared	*Compartí*

Practice! Say everything you read in SPANISH:

Pesé (apples, oranges, grapes)   _____

Congelé (carrots, beans, corn)   _____

Compartí (fruits and vegetables)   _____

ANSWERS:

Compartí las frutas y los vegetales.
Congelé las zanahorias, los frijoles, el maíz.
Pesé las manzanas, las naranjas, las uvas.

You have a lot of words to remember. Connect the sentences that mean the same:

Me gusta la sandía.	I looked at the big chicken.
Guardé el pan blanco.	I drank the cold juice.
Las uvas son buenas.	I prepared my breakfast.
No lavé las papas.	I like the watermelon.
Las naranjas están aquí.	I didn't freeze the butter.
Comí tres huevos.	I put away the white bread.
Bebí el jugo frío.	The oranges are here.
No congelé la mantequilla.	The grapes are good.
Miré el pollo grande.	I ate three eggs.
Preparé mi desayuno.	I didn't wash the potatoes.

ANSWERS:

Me gusta la sandía.	I like the watermelon.
Guardé el pan blanco.	I put away the white bread.
Las uvas son buenas.	The grapes are good.
No lavé las papas.	I didn't wash the potatoes.
Las naranjas están aquí.	The oranges are here.
Comí tres huevos.	I ate three eggs.
Bebí el jugo frío.	I drank the cold juice.
No congelé la mantequilla.	I didn't freeze the butter.
Miré el pollo grande.	I looked at the big chicken.
Preparé mi desayuno.	I prepared my breakfast.

¡Secreto!

You can never learn enough foods in SPANISH.
These are important, too:

sausage	*la salchicha*
beef	*la carne de res*
bacon	*el tocino*
noodles	*los fideos*
rice	*el arroz*

Las bebidas
(Drinks)

Ask your family about what they like to drink. Use this question:

Do you like . . .? *¿Te gusta . . .?*

 lemonade
la limonada

 coffee
el café

 soda
el refresco

 milkshake
el batido

hot chocolate
el chocolate caliente

Sí, me gusta . . .

Which do you like better? Circle your answer:

la limonada o el batido
la leche o el refresco
el chocolate caliente o el café

Más cosas en la cocina
(More things in the kitchen)

Be sure to point out these things in the kitchen today:

pot	*la olla*	knife	*el cuchillo*
frying pan	*el sartén*	fork	*el tenedor*
oven	*el horno*	spoon	*la cuchara*
microwave	*el microondas*	plate	*el plato*
blender	*la licuadora*	glass	*el vaso*
toaster	*la tostadora*	pitcher	*la jarra*

Keep learning new ACTION WORDS! These are also for the kitchen:

I peel	**Pelo**
I peeled	**Pelé**
I peeled the potato.	**Pelé la papa.**

I take	**Tomo**
I took	**Tomé**
I took the frying pan.	**Tomé el sartén.**

I fill	**Lleno**
I filled	**Llené**
I filled the pitcher.	**Llené la jarra.**

I cover	**Cubro**
I covered	**Cubrí**
I covered the pot.	**Cubrí la olla.**

Connect the words that belong together best:

Pelé	**la licuadora**
Llené	**hacia la cocina**
Prendí	**el desayuno**
Preparé	**con el cuchillo**
Caminé	**la jarra**

ANSWERS:

Pelé	*con el cuchillo*
Llené	*la jarra*
Prendí	*la licuadora*
Preparé	*el desayuno*
Caminé	*hacia la cocina*

¿Qué día es hoy?
(What day is today?)

Let's take a break. Use the kitchen calendar to say what day it is:

Today is . . .   *Hoy es . . .*

Monday
Tuesday
Wednesday
Thursday
Friday
Saturday
Sunday

Read these SPANISH words and then answer the questions below in English:

El lunes lavé las papas.
El martes pelé las zanahorias.
El miércoles cociné la sopa.
El jueves mezclé la ensalada.
¡El viernes comí el almuerzo grande!

On what day did you cook the soup?
What happened on Tuesday?
When did you eat the big lunch?
What did you do on Monday?

ANSWERS:

Lavé las papas.	I washed the potatoes.
El viernes	Friday
Pelé las zanahorias.	I peeled the carrots.
El miércoles	Wednesday

Can you tell something you did this week in SPANISH? You can?
¡Muy bien!

¿Cuál es la fecha?
(What's the date?)

Learn to say the date in SPANISH. Start with these:

January *enero*
February *febrero*
March *marzo*

July *julio*
August *agosto*
September *septiembre*

April *abril*
May *mayo*
June *junio*

October *octubre*
November *noviembre*
December *diciembre*

In SPANISH, the number on the calendar goes first:

October <u>5th</u>   el <u>cinco</u> de octubre
May <u>21st</u>   el <u>veinte y uno</u> de mayo
December <u>12th</u>   el <u>doce</u> de diciembre

It's your turn. Go look at the calendar and fill in these two dates:

Hoy es . . .   _____
(Today is . . .)

Ayer fue . . .   _____
(Yesterday was . . .)

¡Secreto!

These are also important!	
week	*la semana*
month	*el mes*
year	*el año*

Now, say these in SPANISH:

June 15th   September 30th   March 22nd

And, answer these questions:

¿Cuántos días en una semana? _____

¿Cuántos meses en un año? _____

ANSWERS:

How many months in a year? 12

How many days in a week? 7

El veinte y dos de marzo
El treinta de septiembre
El quince de junio

Before we leave the kitchen, let's practice our ACTION WORDS. These boys and girls were busy yesterday doing things around the house. Can you write what they said in English?

Yo caminé.   <u>I walked</u>.

Yo corrí. _____

Yo escribí. _____

Yo miré TV. _____

Yo hablé. _____

Yo leí. _____

Yo barrí. _____

Yo comí. _____

ANSWERS:

I ran, I wrote, I watched TV, I spoke, I read, I swept, I ate

Buscapalabras 4
(Word Search 4)

Can you find these words inside the puzzle below?

**comí • escribí • guardé • prendí • caminé
preparé • aprendí • escuché • barrí • corrí**

```
I  L  V  T  R  I  A  E  M  I  S  E  H  N  F
A  I  R  S  G  L  L  S  D  O  H  U  S  E  M
B  Q  E  S  R  F  D  X  M  Z  R  H  N  T  R
C  C  P  R  E  N  D  I  O  E  O  Y  E  O  M
I  D  A  M  T  L  B  C  P  I  R  S  U  V  R
E  G  J  P  S  I  K  W  E  U  O  C  H  K  E
Z  I  U  T  R  A  A  N  M  C  E  O  R  E  N
C  P  E  C  H  E  L  U  I  M  X  K  S  W  O
M  R  S  I  R  M  N  H  E  D  E  U  G  D  I
A  E  C  D  C  I  W  D  H  N  G  S  Q  M  A
T  P  U  P  C  O  R  S  I  N  C  S  P  A  D
O  A  C  W  R  A  R  M  M  V  A  N  A  E  P
S  R  H  R  U  B  A  R  R  I  E  E  I  O  P
R  E  E  G  E  C  O  M  I  S  H  A  T  E  A
E  A  S  P  S  S  X  N  S  A  T  E  X  D  K
```

The answers are on page 129.

The kitchen is full of SPANISH, but there is still more to come.
If you want, read CHAPTER *Cuatro* one more time before
moving ahead. And keep using all the ACTION WORDS!

5 CHAPTER CINCO

Vamos afuera

(Let's go outside)

¿Qué tiempo hace?
(How's the weather?)

It's time to learn SPANISH outside the house.
Start by talking about the weather:

It's . . .	Está . . .
cloudy	*nublado*
snowing	*nevando*
raining	*lloviendo*

It's . . .   *Hace . . .*

cold   hot   sunny
frío   *calor*   *sol*

Now, connect the words that mean the same:

It's snowing.	*Hace sol.*
It's sunny.	*Está lloviendo.*
It's raining.	*Está nevando.*

ANSWERS:

It's raining.	*Está lloviendo.*
It's sunny.	*Hace sol.*
It's snowing.	*Está nevando.*

¡Secreto!

This is how you say that you are cold or hot:

I'm cold.	*Tengo frío.*
I'm hot.	*Tengo calor.*

Más y más acción
(More and more action)

Remember how you changed your ACTION WORDS in SPANISH to talk about what you do <u>every day</u> and what you did <u>yesterday</u>? (See Chapters *Dos*, *Tres*, and *Cuatro*.)

<u>Hablo</u> español en mi casa todos los días.
<u>I speak</u> SPANISH at my house every day.

<u>Hablé</u> español en mi casa ayer.
<u>I spoke</u> SPANISH at my house yesterday.

Well, if you want to talk about <u>what you WILL DO tomorrow</u>, you have to change the last letters of the ACTION WORDS again. Watch:

Mañana <u>hablaré</u> español, <u>leeré</u> mucho
y <u>escribiré</u> en mi libro.
Tomorrow <u>I will speak</u> SPANISH, <u>I will read</u> a lot,
and <u>I will write</u> in my book.

To tell someone what you will do <u>later</u> in SPANISH, the ACTION WORDS end like this:

aré   eré   iré

Try to say each one of these ACTION WORDS:

Hablaré.
I will speak.

Leeré.
I will read.

Escribiré.
I will write.

Caminaré.
I will walk.

Comeré.
I will eat.

Abriré.
I will open.

Escucharé.
I will listen.

Correré.
I will run.

Subiré.
I will go up.

Cocinaré.
I will cook.

Aprenderé.
I will learn.

Viviré.
I will live.

Did you read everything aloud? *¡Muy bien!*

Now you can talk about anything that <u>happens now</u>, that <u>happened before</u>, and that <u>will happen</u> in the future!

I eat chocolate every day.
<u>*Como*</u> *chocolate todos los días.*

I ate chocolate yesterday.
<u>*Comí*</u> *chocolate ayer.*

I will eat chocolate tomorrow.
<u>*Comeré*</u> *chocolate mañana.*

¡Secreto!

To say "not" in SPANISH, JUST SAY ***NO***	
I did not eat chocolate.	***No comí chocolate.***
I will not eat chocolate.	***No comeré chocolate.***

Change these ACTION WORDS from what you will do tomorrow to what you do today:

Caminaré.   _____
I'll walk.   I walk.

Correré.   _____
I'll run.   I run.

Escribiré.   _____
I'll write.   I write.

ANSWERS:
Escribo   Corro   Camino

¡Secreto!

To say what you do <u>every day</u>, what you did <u>yesterday</u>, and what you will do <u>tomorrow</u>, just change the endings!

To talk about . . .	How the ACTION WORD ends:
EVERY DAY	***-o***
YESTERDAY	***-é*** or ***-í***
TOMORROW	***-aré***, ***-eré***, or ***-iré***

El jardín
(The garden)

Go outside. What you will do in the garden?

I will look at the . . . *Miraré . . .*

tree
el árbol

bush
el arbusto

flower
la flor

grass
el pasto

plant
la planta

leaves
las hojas

rocks
las piedras

dirt
la tierra

Draw a picture here of *dos árboles*, *tres flores*,
ocho piedras y cinco arbustos:

¡Secreto!

The little SPANISH word *Hay* means "There is" or "There are." It sounds like the word "I" in English:

There is a lot of dirt.   *Hay mucha tierra.*
There are a lot of rocks.   *Hay muchas piedras.*

73

Put these words in order:

There is a lot of grass in the garden:

en   mucho   Hay   el   jardín   pasto

I will walk toward the big bush.

el   arbusto   hacia   grande   Caminaré

ANSWERS:

Caminaré hacia el arbusto grande.
Hay mucho pasto en el jardín.

Hay acción afuera
(There's action outside)

Add more ACTION WORDS when you go outside.

I will dig	*Cavaré*	I will shout	*Gritaré*
I will plant	*Plantaré*	I will sing	*Cantaré*
I will jump	*Saltaré*	I will swim	*Nadaré*

Tell what <u>you will do</u> today:

_____

_____

_____

Now, connect the words that belong together:

la música   nadaré
las flores   cantaré
el agua   plantaré

ANSWERS:

el agua   nadaré
las flores   plantaré
la música   cantaré

You know lots of ACTION WORDS already. Look at all the things you can do outside today! Connect the sentences with the correct picture:

Subiré el árbol.

Caminaré en el jardín.

Barreré en el patio.

Lavaré el carro.

Correré con mis amigos.

¡Secreto!

These are fun to know, too!

the sun	*el sol*	the wind	*el viento*
the snow	*la nieve*	the storm	*la tormenta*
the clouds	*las nubes*		

Los animales
(Animals)

There are animals outside and in the garden. Can you find the smallest ones?

I will look for the . . .   **Buscaré . . .**

bug	fly	spider	cockroach
el insecto	*la mosca*	*la araña*	*la cucaracha*

ant	bee	worm	snail
la hormiga	*la abeja*	*el gusano*	*el caracol*

Point to these bugs: ***la hormiga***, ***la abeja***, ***la araña***, ***el caracol***

Stop to practice what you learned. Circle the correct answer:

Las hormigas son (cocinas, calcetines, chicas)

La flor es (tierra, pelota, amarilla)

Hace frío y está (mesa, lloviendo, arbusto)

ANSWERS:

chicas
amarilla
lloviendo

And . . . do you have any pets or farm animals? If you do, name them in SPANISH right now:

dog
el perro

cat
el gato

bird
el pájaro

mouse
el ratón

turtle
la tortuga

pig
el puerco

horse
el caballo

cow
la vaca

sheep
la oveja

duck
el pato

Sparky can't find his bone. Will you show him the way?

¡Secreto!

There are wild animals out there, too:

snake	*la culebra*	seal	*la foca*
camel	*el camello*	deer	*el venado*
zebra	*la cebra*	monkey	*el mono*
tiger	*el tigre*	lion	*el león*
wolf	*el lobo*	elephant	*el elefante*

Herramientas
(Tools)

After having fun, help out in the garden. These are some tools you'll need:

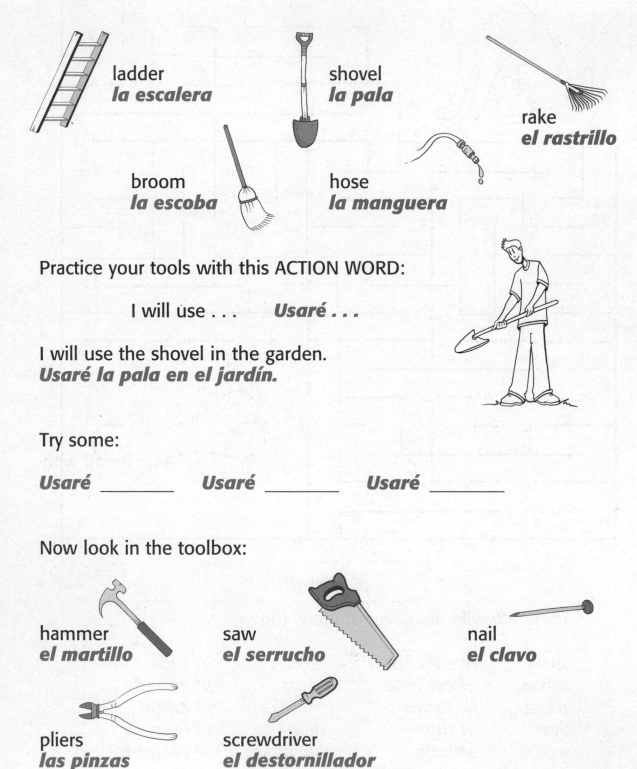

ladder
la escalera

shovel
la pala

rake
el rastrillo

broom
la escoba

hose
la manguera

Practice your tools with this ACTION WORD:

I will use . . .   *Usaré . . .*

I will use the shovel in the garden.
Usaré la pala en el jardín.

Try some:

Usaré _____   *Usaré* _____   *Usaré* _____

Now look in the toolbox:

hammer
el martillo

saw
el serrucho

nail
el clavo

pliers
las pinzas

screwdriver
el destornillador

Circle the word that fits the sentence:

(La escalera, La flor, La oveja) es un animal.
(El serrucho, La tortuga, El árbol) es una herramienta.
(El rastrillo, El arbusto, La vaca) es una planta.

ANSWERS:

la oveja   *el serrucho*   *el arbusto*

Cross out every other letter and read the secret message:

M o e t g o u p s í t r a s m ó i f j m a n r e d o í o n a.

ANSWER:

Me gusta mi jardín. I like my garden.

¡Secreto!

This word has two meanings:

Uso I wear or I use	*Usaré* I'll wear or I'll use

Vamos al centro
(Let's go downtown)

When you are finished in the yard, ask someone to go visit a friend with you. But how will you get there?

I will go by . . .   *Iré en . . .*

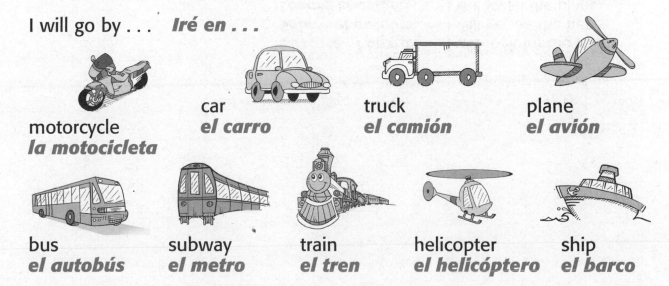

motorcycle
la motocicleta

car
el carro

truck
el camión

plane
el avión

bus
el autobús

subway
el metro

train
el tren

helicopter
el helicóptero

ship
el barco

Fill in the missing letters, and then write the English word:

el _ a _ _ o

la _ ot _ _ ic _ _ ta

_____

_____

el _ u _ o b _ s

el t _ e _

_____

_____

el a _ i _ n

el _ _ t r _

_____

_____

ANSWERS:

el carro (car)   el autobús (bus)   el avión (plane)

la motocicleta (motorcycle)   el tren (train)   el metro (subway)

. Now, connect the sentences that mean the same:

Buscaré el barco.   I will wash the plane.
Subiré el autobús.   I will listen to the train.
Lavaré el avión.   I will look at the truck.
Miraré el camión.   I will look for the ship.
Escucharé el tren.   I will get on the bus.

ANSWERS:

Buscaré el barco.   I will look for the ship.
Subiré el autobús.   I will get on the bus.
Lavaré el avión.   I will wash the plane.
Miraré el camión.   I will look at the truck.
Escucharé el tren.   I will listen to the train.

80

La ciudad
(The city)

When you see one of these, speak out loud in SPANISH:

Let's go to the . . .   *Vamos a . . .*

store
la tienda

restaurant
el restaurante

bank
el banco

street	*la calle*	mailbox	*el buzón*
traffic light	*el semáforo*	church	*la iglesia*
building	*el edificio*	market	*el mercado*
sidewalk	*la acera*	gas station	*la gasolinera*
bridge	*el puente*	school	*la escuela*
sign	*el letrero*		

Okay. Answer these questions in SPANISH:

Where do people keep their money?   <u>*el banco*</u>

Where do people go out to eat?   _____

Where do people cross the river?   _____

Where do people put their mail?   _____

Where do people buy gas for their cars?   _____

ANSWERS:

la gasolinera   *el buzón*   *el puente*   *el restaurante*

¡Secreto!

Learn the words *al* (to the) and *del* (of the):

Let's go <u>to the</u> mailbox.   *Vamos <u>al</u> buzón.*
It's in front <u>of the</u> building.   *Está enfrente <u>del</u> edificio.*

If you visit the city, use words that tell "where."

detrás   **cerca**   **enfrente**   **lejos**
(behind)   (near)   (in front of)   (far from)

1. Put any of these words on the lines below.
2. Read each sentence in SPANISH.
3. Say what it means in English.

El letrero está _____ *del edificio.*
La iglesia está _____ *de la escuela.*
El semáforo está _____ *de la calle.*

Acción en la ciudad
(City action)

Listen to what people are saying in the city. There are new ACTION WORDS everywhere!

I will visit.	*Visitaré.*	*Visitaré el hotel.*
I will drive.	*Manejaré.*	*Manejaré el taxi.*
I will work.	*Trabajaré.*	*Trabajaré mucho.*
I will buy.	*Compraré.*	*Compraré fruta.*
I will call.	*Llamaré.*	*Llamaré mañana.*

What ACTION WORD goes best with each word below?

teléfono   _____
carro   _____
dinero   _____
herramienta   _____
hospital   _____

ANSWERS:

visitaré	*hospital*
trabajaré	*herramienta*
compraré	*dinero*
manejaré	*carro*
llamaré	*teléfono*

Life in the city gets pretty busy sometimes. Listen to people talk about today, yesterday, and tomorrow:

Manejo en la cludad.
No *manejé* ayer,
pero *manejaré* mañana.
(I drive in the city.
I didn't drive yesterday,
but I will drive tomorrow.)

Now, fill in the blanks with the missing words:

Trabajo en la ciudad. No _____ ayer, pero _____ mañana.

Camino en la ciudad. No _____ ayer, pero _____ mañana.

ANSWERS:

caminé, caminaré (I walked, I will walk)
trabajé, trabajaré (I worked, I will work)

¡Secreto!

There are many ways to talk about the FUTURE:

Later	*Más tarde*
I will call later.	*Llamaré más tarde.*
After	*Después de*
I will work after dinner.	*Trabajaré después de la cena.*
Soon	*Pronto*
I will drive soon.	*Manejaré pronto.*

La gente
(People)

The city is a busy place. Say *hola* (hello) to all the people you see:

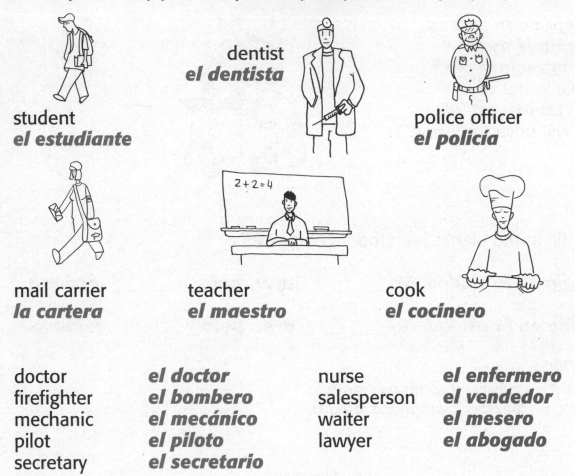

student
el estudiante

dentist
el dentista

police officer
el policía

mail carrier
la cartera

teacher
el maestro

cook
el cocinero

doctor	*el doctor*	nurse	*el enfermero*
firefighter	*el bombero*	salesperson	*el vendedor*
mechanic	*el mecánico*	waiter	*el mesero*
pilot	*el piloto*	lawyer	*el abogado*
secretary	*el secretario*		

Don't forget! Most words that describe girls and women end in the letter *a* and not *o*:

María es una abogada y Susana es una mecánica.
Mary is a lawyer and Susan is a mechanic.

Read this story aloud. What does it mean in English?

La enfermera

Mi nombre es Antonia. Trabajo en el hospital en el centro de la ciudad. Vivo en un apartamento en la ciudad y me gusta mucho. Ayer trabajé, pero mañana es sábado y no trabajaré. Iré a la tienda y compraré zapatos. Uso zapatos blancos en el hospital todos los días.

ANSWER:

The nurse
My name is Antonia. I work at the hospital in the city downtown. I live in an apartment in the city and I like it a lot. I worked yesterday, but tomorrow is Saturday and I will not work. I will go to the store and I will buy shoes. I wear white shoes at the hospital every day.

¡Secreto!

Find these on a map of the United States. You can find more on your own!

Los Angeles (CA)	the angels	*Colorado*	red
Amarillo (TX)	yellow	*Florida*	flowered
Las Cruces (NM)	the crosses	*Montana*	mountain

Now, choose the best way to finish these sentences:

El cartero está	*en el hospital.*
El piloto está	*en el garaje.*
El cocinero está	*en la calle.*
La doctora está	*en el avión.*
El mecánico está	*en el restaurante.*

ANSWERS:

El cartero está en la calle.
El piloto está en el avión.
El cocinero está en el restaurante.
La doctora está en el hospital.
El mecánico está en el garaje.

¿Quién eres tú?
(Who are you?)

As you meet people around town, remember to use the word *Soy* to talk about yourself in SPANISH:

I'm Catalina.
Soy Catalina.

I'm a student.
Soy estudiante.

I'm smart and read a lot of books.
Soy inteligente y leo muchos libros.

Put these words and translate them on the lines below:

Gabriel   bombero
fuerte y manejo un camión grande

Soy _____.   _____

Soy _____.   _____

Soy _____.   _____

ANSWERS:
I'm Gabriel.
I'm a firefighter.
I'm strong and drive a big truck.

Match each question with its answer:

¿Dónde está el semáforo?   Su nombre es Ana.
¿Quién eres tú?   No, es un banco.
¿Quién es la vendedora?   Tres.
¿Es una tienda?   Soy el piloto.
¿Cuántos policías?   En la calle.

ANSWERS:
¿Dónde está el semáforo?   En la calle.
¿Quién eres tú?   Soy el piloto.
¿Quién es la vendedora?   Su nombre es Ana.
¿Es una tienda?   No, es un banco.
¿Cuántos policías?   Tres.

¡Secreto!

The word **eres** is part of many questions:

Are you my friend?	Are you Antonio?	Are you from Cuba?
¿Eres mi amigo?	*¿Eres Antonio?*	*¿Eres de Cuba?*

Más acción afuera
(More action outdoors)

Many boys and girls ride their bikes around town. Try out these new ACTION WORDS today:

I will lift.   **Levantaré.**
             Levantaré mi bicicleta.

I will push.   **Empujaré.**
             Empujaré mi bicicleta.

I will ride.   **Montaré.**
             Montaré mi bicicleta.

I will carry.   **Llevaré.**
             Llevaré mi bicicleta.

I will fix.   **Arreglaré.**
             Arreglaré mi bicicleta.

Circle the ACTIONS that you can do with your bike (there are only three)!

Escucharé	**Viviré**	**Buscaré**
Barreré	**Lavaré**	**Comeré**
Guardaré	**Beberé**	**Cantaré**

ANSWERS:

Buscaré mi bicicleta. (I will look for my bike.)
Lavaré mi bicicleta. (I will wash my bike.)
Guardaré mi bicicleta. (I will put away my bike.)

This time, put the letters in numerical order.
Find out where we're going next in SPANISH:

M(3) *L*(7) *S*(10) *V*(1) *A*(15) *E*(13) *C*(11) *A*(6)

O(4) *A*(2) *E*(9) *U*(12) *A*(8) *S*(5) *L*(14)

ANSWER:

Vamos a la escuela.

Buscapalabras 5
(Word Search 5)

Okay, find these words inside the puzzle below!

*compraré • trabajaré • plantaré • levantaré • montaré
llamaré • llevaré • gritaré • empujaré • cantaré*

É	R	A	T	N	A	C	O	V	O	P
T	J	A	N	R	L	M	U	A	B	C
M	É	O	E	L	É	R	É	É	É	A
C	C	O	M	P	R	A	R	É	M	A
É	E	A	P	T	A	A	R	O	A	L
R	L	A	U	L	T	E	N	L	M	L
A	R	P	J	N	N	T	A	A	J	E
M	T	R	A	B	A	J	A	R	É	V
A	É	V	R	R	L	P	L	U	R	A
L	E	A	É	N	P	L	R	J	N	R
L	É	R	A	T	I	R	G	A	P	É

The answers are on page 130.

Did you finish all the questions and puzzles in this chapter?
¡Qué bueno! Now turn the page and learn more ACTION WORDS . . .

6 CHAPTER SEIS

En la escuela
(At school)

Mi escuela
(My school)

Speak SPANISH on your way to school. And when you get there, what will you do?

Buscaré . . . (I will look for the . . .)

office	*la oficina*
playground	*el campo de recreo*
cafeteria	*la cafetería*
auditorium	*el auditorio*
restrooms	*los servicios*

Practice by putting these words on the lines below:

I'll walk to the _____.
Caminaré a _____.

I'll look at the _____.
Miraré a _____.

I'll point to the _____.
Señalaré a _____.

Now try this question about your school. Just add a number:

What grade are you in?   *¿En qué grado estás?*
I'm in <u>third</u> grade.   *Estoy en el grado <u>tres</u>.*

Now, talk about yourself: *Estoy en el grado _____.*

Acción en la escuela
(Action at school)

Up until now, you have learned how to talk in SPANISH about what you do <u>today</u>, what you did <u>yesterday</u>, and what you will do <u>tomorrow</u>.

Hablo con mis amigos en la clase todos los días.
I talk to my friends in class every day.

Hablé con mis amigos en la clase ayer.
I talked to my friends in class yesterday.

Hablaré con mis amigos en la clase mañana.
I will talk to my friends in class tomorrow.

Keep reading aloud:

Escucho a la maestra.	I listen to the teacher.
Escuché a la maestra.	I listened to the teacher.
Escucharé a la maestra.	I'll listen to the teacher.
Como en los bancos.	I eat on the benches.
Comí en los bancos.	I ate on the benches.
Comeré en los bancos.	I will eat on the benches.

Now learn this important ACTION WORD:

I study every day.	<u>*Estudio*</u> *todos los días.*
I studied yesterday.	<u>*Estudié*</u> *ayer.*
I will study tomorrow.	<u>*Estudiaré*</u> *mañana.*

The ACTION WORDS below are missing some final letters. Fill each line with the correct word ending:

$$\boxed{\text{-o} \qquad \text{-í} \qquad \text{-aré}}$$

I <u>walk</u> to school every day.
Camin__ a la escuela todos los días.

I <u>ran</u> to school yesterday.
Corr__ a la escuela ayer.

I <u>will ride</u> my bike to school tomorrow.
Mont__ mi bicicleta a la escuela mañana.

ANSWERS:

Montaré
Corrí
Camino

¡Secreto!

REMEMBER: To tell <u>when</u> something happens, change the last letters of the ACTION WORD:

I do it everyday (*o*, like *Estudi<u>o</u>*).
I did it yesterday (*é* or *í*, like *Estudi<u>é</u>*).
I will do it tomorrow (*aré*, *eré*, or *iré*, like *Estudi<u>aré</u>*).

Mi salón de clase
(My classroom)

It's time to practice SPANISH in the classroom:

I look at the . . .   *Miro . . .*

desk
el escritorio

flag
la bandera

pencil sharpener
el sacapuntas

I have the . . .   *Tengo . . .*

backpack
la mochila

paper
el papel

pencil
el lápiz

pen
el lapicero

eraser
el borrador

notebook
el cuaderno

And now, circle the one word that doesn't belong:

el lápiz, el lapicero, la bicicleta
el libro, el auditorio, el cuaderno
escritorio, estudio, escucho

ANSWERS:
la bicicleta, el auditorio, escritorio

93

¿Qué necesitas?
(What do you need?)

Tell everyone in the class what you need in SPANISH:

I need the . . .   *Necesito . . .*

crayons
los gises

paintbrush
la brocha

glue
el pegamento

scissors
las tijeras

marker
el marcador

ruler
la regla

Connect each picture with the proper word:

las tijeras   *los gises*   *el pegamento*   *el marcador*

Now answer this question by writing *all* the school words in SPANISH you can remember:

¿Qué necesitas?

Necesito _____   _____   _____

_____   _____   _____

_____   _____   _____

_____   _____   _____

Ready to learn more ACTION WORDS for school?

EVERY DAY	YESTERDAY	TOMORROW
Corto (I cut)	*Corté* (I did cut)	*Cortaré* (I'll cut)
Pinto (I color)	*Pinté* (I colored)	*Pintaré* (I'll color)
Dibujo (I draw)	*Dibujé* (I drew)	*Dibujaré* (I'll draw)

Practice by finishing this in SPANISH:

I cut with the scissors, I color with the crayons, and I draw with the marker.

Corto con las tijeras, _____, y _____.

ANSWERS:
dibujo con el marcador.
pinto con los gises

You learned these words before, so write what they mean in English:

la computadora   _____
el reloj   _____
el libro   _____
el bote de basura   _____
el gabinete   _____

ANSWERS:
computer, clock, book, trashcan, cabinet

¡Secreto!

When something belongs to someone, use *de* (it means "of"):

It is Victor's pencil.   *Es el lápiz de Victor.*
It is the teacher's desk.   *Es el escritorio del maestro.*

Mi clase
(My class)

What class do you like best?

I like . . .   *Me gusta . . .*

music
la música

art
el arte

science
la ciencia

math	*las matemáticas*
social studies	*los estudios sociales*
language	*el lenguaje*
history	*la historia*

Which of these words go together? Draw a line:

los gises	*la ciencia*
los números	*el lenguaje*
el piano	*el arte*
los animales	*las matemáticas*
el español	*la música*

ANSWERS:

el arte	*los gises*
las matemáticas	*los números*
la música	*el piano*
la ciencia	*los animales*
el lenguaje	*el español*

96

Más acción en la escuela
(More action at school)

Here's an ACTION WORD you must learn right away:

I learn	**Aprendo**
I learned	**Aprendí**
I will learn	**Aprenderé**

Put your favorite **clase** on the lines below:

I learn every day.   **Aprendo _____ todos los días.**

I learned yesterday.   **Aprendí _____ ayer.**

I will learn tomorrow.   **Aprenderé _____ mañana.**

All over the school, kids are saying what they do. Use this to practice these new ACTION WORDS:

I ask	**Pregunto**
I asked	**Pregunté**
I'll ask	**Preguntaré**
. . . the teacher	**. . . a la maestra.**

I answer	**Contesto**
I answered	**Contesté**
I'll answer	**Contestaré**
. . . the teacher	**. . . al maestro.**

97

El mundo
(The world)

I'll look for the . . . **"Buscaré . . ."**

state	**el estado**
country	**el país**
world	**el mundo**

Okay, fill in the blanks with the right words:

desierto, lago, montañas, bosque, mundo

Miro muchos árboles en el _____.

Subo y bajo las _____.

Nado en el _____.

Bebo mucha agua en el _____.

Estudio los países del _____.

ANSWERS:

Miro muchos árboles en el bosque.
Subo y bajo las montañas.
Nado en el lago.
Bebo mucha agua en el desierto.
Estudio los países del mundo.

This time, say where you live:

Vivo en la calle _____. (your street)

Vivo en la ciudad de _____. (your town)

Vivo en el estado de _____. (your state)

As you learn about the world, use these great ACTION WORDS:

I travel.	*Viajo.*
I traveled.	*Viajé.*
I will travel.	*Viajaré.*

Some day I will travel to many different countries.
Algún día viajaré a muchos países diferentes.

¡Secreto!

Do you know where to find these on a map? There are many places in the world where the kids speak only SPANISH!

English *(inglés)*
United States *(Estados Unidos)*   Canada *(Canadá)*
England *(Inglaterra)*   New Zealand *(Nueva Zelanda)*

Spanish *(español)*
España (Spain)   *El Salvador   Puerto Rico   Bolivia
Uruguay   México   Santo Domingo   Panamá
Guatemala   Colombia   Argentina   Paraguay
Costa Rica   Chile   Nicaragua   Ecuador
República Dominicana   Perú   Venezuela   Honduras*

El campo de recreo
(The playground)

After school, have some fun in SPANISH. Say different words when you play with your friends:

Let's go to the . . .   *Vamos a . . .*

seesaw   swing   slide
el subibaja   *el columpio*   *el resbalador*

merry-go-round   bars   court   field
los caballitos *las barras*   *la cancha*   *el campo*

Fill in the missing letters:

el _ e _ _ a l _ _ o _   el _ o _ u _ p _ o

el _ _ b i _ a _ _

You learned to name these things earlier. Write in the English:

Necesito . . .   I need the . . .

el bate   <u>bat</u>

la pelota   _____

el guante   _____

la bicicleta   _____

la patineta   _____

el juguete   _____

ANSWERS:

el resbalador, el columpio, el subibaja
ball, glove, bike, skateboard, toy

What else will you do on the playground?

Subiré al subibaja.
I will get on the seesaw.

Montaré los caballitos.
I will ride the merry-go-round.

Empujaré el columpio.
I will push the swing.

These three new ACTION WORDS let you talk about playing with a ball. You can use them <u>today</u>, <u>yesterday</u>, and <u>tomorrow</u>, too. Go ahead, make full sentences all by yourself!

Pateo (I kick)   <u>**la pelota todos los días.**</u>
Pateé (I kicked)   <u>**la pelota ayer.**</u>
Patearé (I'll kick)   <u>**la pelota mañana.**</u>

Tiro (I throw)   _____

Tiré (I threw)   _____

Tiraré (I'll throw)   _____

Agarro (I catch)   _____

Agarré (I caught)   _____

Agarraré (I'll catch)   _____

And what did you do at school yesterday? Choose the best match:

Bajé	**el almuerzo**
Agarré	**con el pie**
Pateé	**con el guante**
Corrí	**a la cancha**
Comí	**del resbalador**

ANSWERS:

Bajé *del resbalador.*	**Comí** *el almuerzo.*
Agarré *con el guante.*	**Corrí** *a la cancha.*
Pateé *con el pie.*	

Los juegos
(The games)

The ACTION WORD "play" is **jugar**, but when you talk about playing, it changes a little:

Juego (I play)

Jugué (I played)

Jugaré (I'll play)

I'll play . . . **Jugaré** . . .

basketball	**el baloncesto**	tag	**la pega**
baseball	**el béisbol**	jump rope	**la soga**
soccer	**el fútbol**	dodge ball	**el quemado**

Put the words in each sentence in the right order:

campo Jugué fútbol en de el
<u>*Jugué en el campo de fútbol*</u>.

la soga el Salto de juego en
_____

en blanco un casa Tengo béisbol mi
_____

You made noise while playing yesterday. Say what you did, in SPANISH:

Hablé _____.   *Grité* _____.   *Canté* _____.

Now, write your favorite game on the line below:

I like _____ a lot.   *Me gusta* _____ *mucho.*

ANSWERS:

¡Muy importante!
(Very important!)

Usted and *tú* both mean "you." Say *usted* to your teacher instead of *tú*. Use *tú* only with your family and friends. Look at the difference:

How are <u>you</u>, my friend?
¿Cómo estás <u>tú</u>, mi amigo?

How are <u>you</u>, teacher?
¿Cómo está <u>usted</u>, maestro?

Más diversión
(More fun)

Kids are having fun all over the place. Underline the ones you like best:

I like . . .   *Me gusta . . .*

wrestling	*la lucha*
reading	*la lectura*
dancing	*el baile*

I want . . .   *Quiero . . .*

cartoons	*los dibujos animados*
jokes	*los chistes*
stories	*los cuentos*
tricks	*los trucos*
puzzles	*los rompecabezas*

I'll go to the . . .   *Iré a . . .*

movies	*el cine*
park	*el parque*
zoo	*el zoológico*

Which word does not belong with the other three?

cuentos, lectura, leer, columpio
cine, juego, zoológico, parque
trucos, barras, rompecabezas, chistes

ANSWERS:
barras
juego
columpio

Look at this CROSSWORD puzzle. Put these words in SPANISH in the spaces below:

Palabras Cruzadas 1

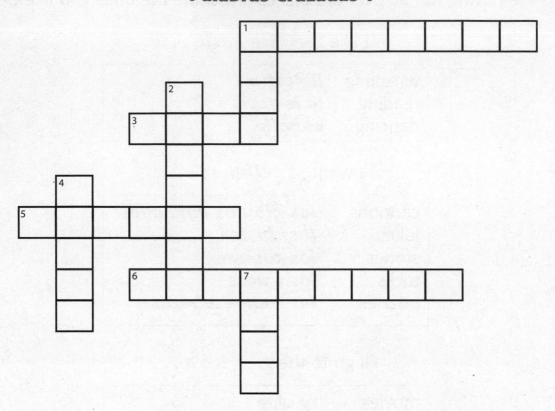

ACROSS:
1. seesaw
3. tag
5. park
6. songs

DOWN:
1. jump rope
2. reading
4. dancing
7. movies

Find the answers on page 130.

¡La fiesta!
(The party!)

Let's have a party at school. Talk about it in SPANISH:

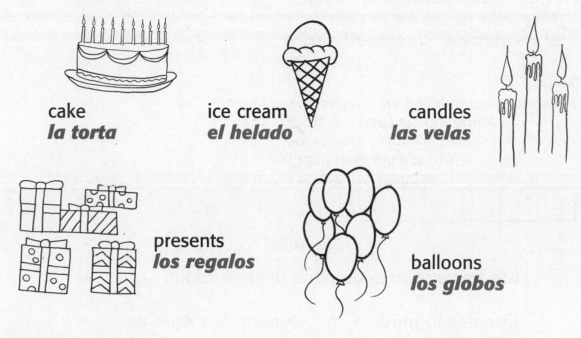

cake
la torta

ice cream
el helado

candles
las velas

presents
los regalos

balloons
los globos

Practice:

I ate the ice cream.	***Comí _____.***
I like the gift.	***Me gusta _____.***
I'll take the cake.	***Llevaré _____.***
I'll look for the candles.	***Buscaré _____.***
I played with the balloons.	***Jugué con _____.***

Here are more ***fiesta*** words that you should know. Say them in SPANISH:

la limonada y los refrescos
mi familia y mis amigos
la música y el baile

ANSWERS:

el helado, el regalo, la torta, las velas, los globos
the lemonade and the soft drinks
my family and my friends
the music and the dancing

Try this conversation. But first, say what it means in English:

#1 *Hoy es mi cumpleaños.*
#2 *¡Qué bueno! ¿Cuántos años tienes?*
#1 *Tengo once. Estoy muy feliz.*
#2 *¿Hay una fiesta en tu casa?*
#1 *Sí, y vamos al cine en la noche.*

ANSWERS:

#1 Today is my birthday.
#2 Great! How old are you?
#1 I'm eleven. I am very happy.
#2 Is there a party at your house?
#1 Yes, and we are going to the movies at night.

¡Secreto!

> Maybe you like to do other things for fun:
>
> | listening to music | *escuchar música* |
> | bike riding | *montar en bicicleta* |
> | watching movies | *ver películas* |
> | hanging out with friends | *estar con los amigos* |
> | exercising | *hacer ejercicio* |

Now name a few more party snacks:

I want . . . *Quiero . . .*

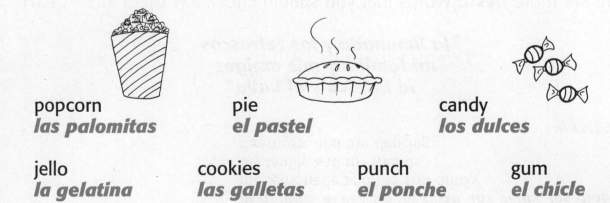

popcorn	pie	candy
las palomitas	*el pastel*	*los dulces*

jello	cookies	punch	gum
la gelatina	*las galletas*	*el ponche*	*el chicle*

Draw a line between the words that match best:

las galletas	*el pastel*
la música	*la fruta*
el ponche	*los dulces*
el maíz	*el baile*
la torta	*las palomitas*

ANSWERS:

el pastel	*la torta*
las palomitas	*el maíz*
la fruta	*el ponche*
el baile	*la música*
los dulces	*las galletas*

And don't forget to say these things in SPANISH at your next big party:

Welcome!	*¡Bienvenido!*
Congratulations!	*¡Felicitaciones!*
Good luck!	*¡Buena suerte!*

Buscapalabras 6
(Word Search 6)

And now, find these words inside the puzzle below!

agarro • aprendo • contesto • corto • dibujo
estudio • juego • pateo • pinto • pregunto • tiro

```
F N D O D R P L J W T W C O V
O I H P D A P U P Q U O H J Y
U E A R J N E S Z W N E P U S
B W Z E I G E C H T N T O B X
W T E G O I N R E E B R U I J
O I D U T S E S P O R I T D M
P W E N W I T Q E A G B E T P
E I R T D O P R G C O R T O A
K V N O J B A A M U R Y Z B T
D A H T O P D U W P P I X Q E
Z V N T O J B Y H L Q Y J H O
G Z X A F P M B H H C G N G N
```

The answers are on page 130.

Wow! You learned a lot today. Now, let's hurry home after school—
to learn more ACTION WORDS . . .

7 CHAPTER
SIETE

La noche
(Nighttime)

Ayudo en la casa
(I help in the house)

Once you get home from school, help around the house. First, use SPANISH to set the table:

I need the . . .
Necesito . . .

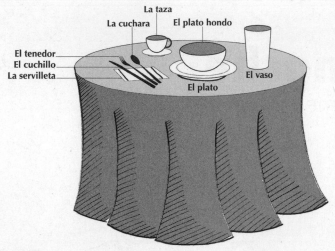

La cuchara
La taza
El plato hondo
El tenedor
El cuchillo
La servilleta
El plato
El vaso

Connect the words that go together:

la taza	*el tenedor*
la silla	*el platillo*
la cuchara	*la mesa*

ANSWERS:

la taza — el platillo
la silla — la mesa
la cuchara — el tenedor

Now learn these two new ACTION WORDS. After you set the table, read all the SPANISH aloud!

Ayudo. (I help.)
Ayudo en la casa.
Ayudé. (I helped.)
Ayudé en la casa ayer.
Ayudaré. (I'll help.)
Ayudaré en la casa mañana.

Limpio. (I clean.)
Limpio la cocina.
Limpié. (I cleaned.)
Limpié la cocina ayer.
Limpiaré. (I'll clean.)
Limpiaré la cocina mañana.

Palabras especiales
(Special words)

Some SPANISH ACTION WORDS are very <u>special</u>. They look different from the ones we learned earlier in this book.

Look! This one changes a lot when you talk about every day, yesterday, or tomorrow:

Pongo. (I put.)
Todos los días <u>pongo</u> los platos en la mesa.
Every day I put the plates on the table.

Puse. (I did put.)
Ayer <u>puse</u> los platos en la mesa.
Yesterday I put the plates on the table.

Pondré. (I'll put.)
Mañana <u>pondré</u> los platos en la mesa.
Tomorrow I'll put the plates on the table.

See? The others only change a little at the end:

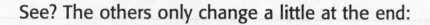

I study.	**Estudio.** (ends in **o**)
I studied.	**Estudié.** (ends in **é** or **í**)
I will study.	**Estudiaré.** (ends in **aré**, **eré**, or **iré**)

¡Secreto!

HERE ARE MORE VERY <u>SPECIAL</u> ACTION WORDS.
THEY ARE <u>SPECIAL</u> BECAUSE THEY CHANGE A LOT!

Voy. (I go.)   **Fui.** (I went.)   **Iré.** (I'll go.)
Vengo. (I come.)   **Vine.** (I came.)   **Vendré.** (I'll come.)
Doy. (I give.)   **Di.** (I gave.)   **Daré.** (I'll give.)

Do you think you can make SPANISH sentences with them?
Give it a try, translate:

I help a lot in my house. _____

I went to the kitchen. _____

I (did) put the napkins on the table. _____

ANSWERS:

Puse las servilletas en la mesa.
Fui a la cocina.
Ayudo mucho en mi casa.

Now, connect the sentences that mean the same:

Let's go to the kitchen.	*Guardaré las tazas nuevas.*
I put the fork here.	*Tengo la servilleta roja.*
I'll take two big plates.	*Lavé el plato hondo blanco.*
The glass is not on the table.	*Vamos a la cocina.*
I'll put away the new cups.	*El vaso no está en la mesa.*
I have the red napkin.	*Pongo el tenedor aquí.*
I washed the white bowl.	*Llevaré dos platos grandes.*

ANSWERS:

Lavé el plato hondo blanco.	I washed the white bowl.
Tengo la servilleta roja.	I have the red napkin.
Guardaré las tazas nuevas.	I'll put away the new cups.
El vaso no está en la mesa.	The glass is not on the table.
Llevaré dos platos grandes.	I'll take two big plates.
Pongo el tenedor aquí.	I put the fork here.
Vamos a la cocina.	Let's go to the kitchen.

¡Limpio todo!
(I clean everything!)

After dinner, clean up around the house. Begin with what you already know. Write in the missing words:

I will wash the chair with water.
Lavaré la silla con _____.

I will sweep the floor with the broom.
Barreré el piso con _____.

I will put the paper in the trashcan.
Meteré el papel en _____.

ANSWERS:
agua, la escoba, el bote de basura

This time, say something different:

I'll use the . . .   *Usaré . . .*

mop	*el trapeador*	bucket	*el balde*
sponge	*la esponja*	soap	*el jabón*
towel	*la toalla*		

Write the word to match each number below:

1. _____ 2. _____ 3. _____ 4. _____ 5. _____

ANSWERS:
1. el trapeador 2. el balde 3. la esponja 4. la toalla 5. el jabón

Keep cleaning the house in SPANISH. These <u>special</u> ACTION WORDS will help:

I pick up	*Recojo*	
I picked up	*Recogí*	*la esponja.*
I'll pick up	*Recogeré*	

I move	*Muevo*	
I moved	*Moví*	*el balde.*
I'll move	*Moveré*	

Which cleaning tools always go together?

Break this code to find the answer:

1	2	3	4	5	6	7	8	9	10	11	12	13
A	B	C	D	E	F	G	H	I	J	K	L	M

14	15	16	17	18	19	20	21	22	23	24	25
N	O	P	Q	R	S	T	U	V	W	X	Y

5–12–2–1–12–4–5–25–5–12–20–18–1–16–5–1–4–15–18

ANSWER:
el balde y el trapeador

¡*Secreto!*

> Here are more things you can say:
>
> It's clean. *Está limpio.*
> It's dirty. *Está sucio.*

114

El baño
(The bathroom)

Cleaning the house can be dirty work!

I cleaned the . . .   *Limpié* . . .

sink
el lavabo

mirror
el espejo

faucet
el grifo

bathtub
la tina

shower
la ducha

toilet
el excusado

Cross out the one word that doesn't belong:

la escuela, la tina, la ducha, el lavabo
recojo, canto, muevo, levanto
el cuchillo, el agua, el jabón, la esponja

ANSWERS:

el cuchillo   *canto*   *la escuela*

Put the words in these sentences in order, and write what they mean in English:

miro baño la al y ducha Voy

_____

lavabo Pongo caliente el en agua el

_____

la Uso y tina limpio esponja la

_____

ANSWERS:

Voy al baño y miro la ducha.
I go to the bathroom and I look at the shower.
Pongo el agua caliente en el lavabo.
I put the hot water in the sink.
Uso la esponja y limpio la tina.
I use the sponge and I clean the bathtub.

115

Did you get them all right? *Muy bien.* Now, point!

I want the . . .   *Quiero . . .*

hairbrush	*el cepillo*
comb	*el peine*
toothbrush	*el cepillo de dientes*
toothpaste	*la pasta de dientes*
deodorant	*el desodorante*

Underline the correct word:

El peine es (guapo, viejo, plátano).
Guardé mi cepillo en el (libro, piso, baño).
Puse el balde en la (ducha, oveja, camisa).
La pasta de dientes es (arte, leche, verde).
Limpié el espejo y el (helado, clavo, lavabo).

ANSWERS:
viejo, baño, ducha, verde, lavabo

Mi cuerpo
(My body)

As long as you are in the bathroom, why not take a bath in SPANISH!
Say each part as you scrub:

I wash my . . .   *Me lavo . . .*

head	*la cabeza*
neck	*el cuello*
shoulder	*el hombro*
arm	*el brazo*
chest	*el pecho*
hand	*la mano*
back	*la espalda*
stomach	*el estómago*
leg	*la pierna*
foot	*el pie*

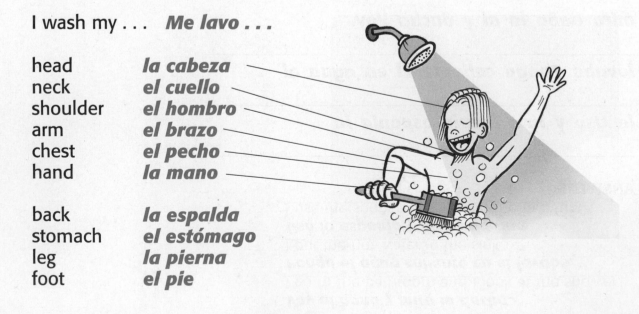

Put these letters in order:

m o h o r b   _____

r i n e a p   _____

d a p e s a l   _____

z a a c e b   _____

l o c u l e   _____

h o p e c   _____

ANSWERS:

hombro, pierna, espalda, cabeza, cuello, pecho

¡Secreto!

> This <u>special</u> ACTION WORD means "I wash my":
>
> *Me lavo*
>
> I wash my hands.   *Me lavo las manos.*

Look in the mirror and say each one of these out loud:

hair	*el pelo*
eye	*el ojo*
nose	*la nariz*
ear	*la oreja*
mouth	*la boca*
teeth	*los dientes*
face	*la cara*

Now, practice these with another <u>special</u> ACTION WORD:

Veo (I see)   <u>*Veo la nariz.*</u>

Vi (I saw)   <u>*Vi los ojos.*</u>

Veré (I'll see)   <u>*Veré la boca.*</u>

Here comes a tough exercise! Look at the three sentences below and translate them into English. Do you think you can do it?

Miré en el espejo y vi dientes blancos.

_____

Miro en el espejo y veo una cara bonita.

_____

Miraré en el espejo y veré una persona inteligente.

_____

ANSWERS:

I looked in the mirror and saw white teeth.
I look in the mirror and see a pretty face.
I will look in the mirror and I will see a smart person.

¡Estoy enfermo! ¡Estoy enferma!
(I'm sick)

What's wrong with you?

It's a . . .	*Es . . .*
cough	*la tos*
cold	*el resfriado*
fever	*la fiebre*

I have a . . .	*Tengo un . . .*
stomachache	*dolor de estómago*
headache	*dolor de cabeza*
toothache	*dolor de muela*

Talk in SPANISH when you don't feel well:

I need the . . .	Necesito . . .
aspirin	*la aspirina*
Band–aid®	*la curita*
medicine	*la medicina*
thermometer	*el termómetro*
vitamin	*la vitamina*

Connect the words that belong together:

dolor de cabeza	*el dentista*
dolor de estómago	*una aspirina*
dolor de muela	*cinco hamburguesas*

ANSWERS:

dolor de muela   *el dentista*
dolor de estómago   *cinco hamburguesas*
dolor de cabeza   *una aspirina*

¡Secreto!

> **¿Qué te pasa?** means "What's the matter?"
>
> **Me duele** means "It hurts."

A la cama
(Off to bed)

Climb into bed and practice your SPANISH there. This is a <u>special</u> ACTION WORD that you'll need:

Duermo (I sleep)	*en mi dormitorio.*
Dormí (I slept)	*toda la noche.*
Dormiré (I'll sleep)	*con el español en la cabeza.*

You spoke SPANISH everywhere you went! Read through some of the things you did, and write the same sentences in English:

Bajé de la cama.   I got out of bed.

Caminé por la casa.   _____

Preparé mi desayuno.   _____

Planté flores en el jardín.   _____

Monté mi bicicleta.   _____

Estudié en la escuela.   _____

Jugué con mis amigos.   _____

Ayudé en la casa.   _____

ANSWERS:

I helped in the house.
I played with my friends.
I studied at school.
I rode my bike.
I planted flowers in the garden.
I prepared my breakfast.
I walked through the house.

¡Buenas noches!
(Good night!)

Before you fall asleep, look out the window and talk about the sky at night:

I look at the . . .   *Miro . . .*

star	moon	planet	comet
la estrella	*la luna*	*el planeta*	*el cometa*

space	*el espacio*	satellite	*el satélite*
telescope	*el telescopio*	spaceship	*la nave espacial*

Put any of these words on the lines below. Then, read the full sentence in SPANISH:

Señalo _____.
Veo _____.
Busco _____.

You will know how to make a lot of sentences if you learn these other ACTION WORDS:

Digo (I say) **Dije** (I said) **Diré** (I'll say)

Oigo (I hear) **Oí** (I heard) **Oiré** (I'll hear)

Traigo (I bring) **Traje** (I brought) **Traeré** (I'll bring)

These words are all mixed up and bunched together. Separate and rearrange them:

"hola"aDigoamigosmis. _____
enmimúsicacuartoOigo. _____
acamalaTraigolibroel. _____

¡Secreto!

Do you like nighttime? Why not say these in SPANISH:

It's dark.	*Está oscuro.*
I'm not afraid.	*No tengo miedo.*
Are you afraid?	*¿Tienes miedo tú?*

El libro de cuentos
(The storybook)

It's late, so take out your favorite storybook. Name these characters *en español*:

I like the . . .   *Me gusta . . .*

princess   king
la princesa   *el rey*

              wizard   ghost
              el mago   *el fantasma*

Here is the . . .   *Aquí tienes . . .*

monster   witch
el monstruo   *la bruja*

        dragon   elf
        el dragón   *el duende*

Answer with "T" for TRUE and "F" for FALSE:

El duende es más grande que el gigante.   _____
La hija del rey es la princesa.   _____
Las brujas son muy bonitas.   _____

ANSWERS:
F, T, F

Draw a line from these words to each picture:

comeré

barro

monté

ANSWERS:

(comeré) I'll eat.
(barro) I sweep.
(monté) I rode.

Okay, fill in these words inside the crossword below!

Palabras Cruzadas 2

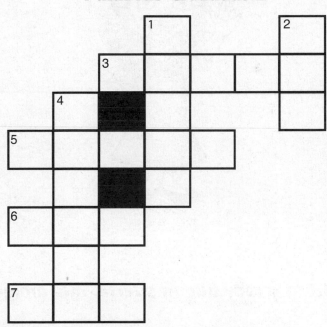

ACROSS:
3. I come
5. I play
6. I see
7. I give

DOWN:
1. I have
2. I go
4. I want

Did you finish the crossword? *¡Muy bien!*
Find the answers on page 130.

Antes de irte
(Before you go)

. . . And now, think about it! You KNOW SPANISH!

Isn't it awesome? You can speak SPANISH to Hispanic friends and their families any time you want!

But you must remember everything you learned. Tomorrow turn to Chapter *Uno* and read this book again so that everything stays and you can have more fun with . . . **SPANISH EVERY DAY—ACTION WORDS!**

¡Adiós y muy buena suerte, mis amigos!

My Daily Checklist

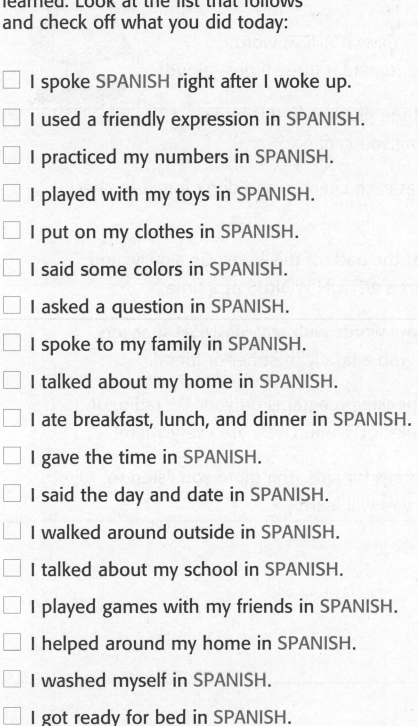

Here's something that will help you remember all the SPANISH you have learned. Look at the list that follows and check off what you did today:

☐ I spoke SPANISH right after I woke up.

☐ I used a friendly expression in SPANISH.

☐ I practiced my numbers in SPANISH.

☐ I played with my toys in SPANISH.

☐ I put on my clothes in SPANISH.

☐ I said some colors in SPANISH.

☐ I asked a question in SPANISH.

☐ I spoke to my family in SPANISH.

☐ I talked about my home in SPANISH.

☐ I ate breakfast, lunch, and dinner in SPANISH.

☐ I gave the time in SPANISH.

☐ I said the day and date in SPANISH.

☐ I walked around outside in SPANISH.

☐ I talked about my school in SPANISH.

☐ I played games with my friends in SPANISH.

☐ I helped around my home in SPANISH.

☐ I washed myself in SPANISH.

☐ I got ready for bed in SPANISH.

Powerful Practice Tips

1. When you come to a new SPANISH word in this book, be sure to read it three times—aloud!

2. Touch and name all the pictures in this book. Then, color everything you can.

3. Do all the activities in each chapter, and don't forget to check your answers.

4. Use the flashcards at the back of this book. Go slowly, and only learn two or three ACTION WORDS at a time.

5. If you can, try out new words with real SPANISH speakers. Otherwise, practice with a family member or friend.

6. Look for SPANISH-speaking programs on your TV, radio, or computer. Great books, CDs, and DVDs are everywhere!

7. Listen to SPANISH songs for kids. The more you listen to SPANISH, the faster you will learn.

Spanish Culture

People who live in Spanish-speaking countries do many things differently than we do here in the United States. That is because they have a different **culture**. A **culture** includes things like the way people live, what they eat, and how they dress. You can learn more about **culture** in books or on the Internet. But, the best way to learn about people is to talk to them. When you get the chance, talk to as many Spanish-speaking people as you can. Soon you will know more than the Spanish language—you will understand the **culture**, too!

A Spanish Song

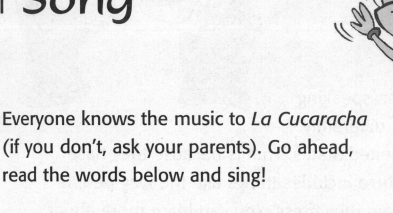

Everyone knows the music to *La Cucaracha* (if you don't, ask your parents). Go ahead, read the words below and sing!

la cucaracha,   **la cucaracha**
(lah koo-kah-RAH-chah)   (lah koo-kah-RAH-chah)
The cockroach, the cockroach

ya   **no**   **puede**   **caminar**
(yah   noh   PWEH-deh   kah-mee-NAHR)
can't walk anymore,

porque   **le**   **falta**
(POHR-keh   leh   FAHL-tah)
because he's missing,

porque   **no**   **tiene**
(POHR-keh   noh   tee-YEH-neh)
because he doesn't have

una   **pata**   **para**   **andar**
(OO-nah   PAH-tah   PAH-rah   ahn-DAHR)
a leg to walk on!

128

Answers

Buscapalabras 1

Buscapalabras 3

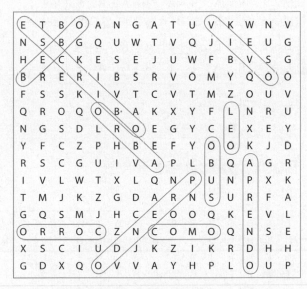

Buscapalabras 2

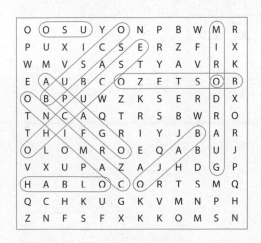

Buscapalabras 4

Buscapalabras 5

Palabras Cruzadas 1

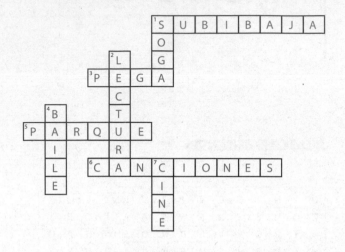

Buscapalabras 6

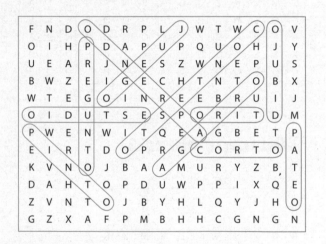

Palabras Cruzadas 2

English–Spanish Vocabulary List

Note that some Spanish words may be masculine or feminine. Masculine words require the masculine "the" (**el**)—for example, "the truck" is **el camión**. Feminine words have to be used with the feminine "the" (**la**)—for example, "the house" is **la casa**.

A masculine word will combine with other masculine words in a sentence; for example, **el camión blanco**. A feminine word will combine with feminine words in a sentence; for example, **la casa blanca**.

ENGLISH	ESPAÑOL
a	**un** or **una**
a little bit	**poquito**
a lot	**mucho**
above	**encima**
address	**la dirección**
after	**después**
all	**todo** or **toda**
almost	**casi**
always	**siempre**
American	**americano** or **americana**
an	**un** or **una**
and	**y**
angel	**el ángel**
angry	**enojado** or **enojada**
animal	**el animal**
another	**otro** or **otra**
ant	**la hormiga** ◄
apartment	**el apartamento**
apple	**la manzana**
April	**abril**
arm	**el brazo**
armchair	**el sillón** ◄
art	**el arte**
aspirin	**la aspirina**
astronaut	**el** or **la astronauta**
at	**en**
attic	**el desván**
August	**agosto**
aunt	**la tía** ◄
baby	**el bebé**
back	**la espalda**
backpack	**la mochila**
bad	**malo** or **mala**
bag	**la bolsa**
ball	**la pelota**
balloon	**el globo**
banana	**el plátano** ◄
Band-aid®	**la curita**
bank	**el banco**
bars	**las barras**
baseball	**el béisbol** ▲
basement	**el sótano**
basketball	**el baloncesto**
bat	**el bate**
bathroom	**el baño**
bathtub	**la tina**

131

beach	**la playa**	bulletin board	**el tablero de anuncios**	
beans	**los frijoles**			
bed	**la cama** ◄	bus	**el autobús**	
bedroom	**el dormitorio**	bush	**el arbusto**	
bedspread	**la cubrecama**	but	**pero**	
bee	**la abeja**	butter	**la mantequilla**	
before	**antes**			
behind	**detrás**	cabinet	**el gabinete**	
bell	**la campana**	cake	**la torta** ◄	
belt	**el cinturón**	calendar	**el calendario**	
benches	**los bancos**	camera	**la cámara**	

		candles	**las velas**	
		candy	**los dulces**	
		cap	**la gorra**	
bicycle	**la bicicleta** ▲	car	**el carro** ◄	
big	**grande**	carpet	**la alfombra**	
bird	**el pájaro**	carrot	**la zanahoria**	
black	**negro** or **negra**	cartoons	**los dibujos animados**	
blackboard	**el pizarrón**	cat	**el gato** or **la gata**	
blanket	**la frazada**	ceiling	**el techo**	
blocks	**los bloques**	celery	**el apio**	
blouse	**la blusa** ◄	chair	**la silla** ◄	
blue	**azul**	chalk	**la tiza**	
boat	**el bote**	chapter	**el capítulo**	
body	**el cuerpo**	cheap	**barato** or **barata**	
book	**el libro**	checkers	**el juego de damas**	
bookshelf	**el librero**	cheese	**el queso**	
boots	**las botas**	chest	**el pecho**	
bottle	**la botella**	chicken	**el pollo** ◄	
bowl	**el plato hondo**	children	**los niños**	
box	**la caja**	chimney	**la chimenea**	
boy	**el niño** ◄	chocolate	**el chocolate** ◄	
bracelet	**el brazalete**	church	**la iglesia**	
brave	**valiente**	city	**la ciudad**	
bread	**el pan**	class	**la clase**	
breakfast	**el desayuno**	classroom	**el salón de clase**	
bridge	**el puente**	clean	**limpio** or **limpia**	
broom	**la escoba**	clock	**el reloj**	
brother	**el hermano**	closed	**cerrado** or **cerrada**	
brown	**café**	closet	**el ropero** ◄	
bucket	**el balde**	clothes	**la ropa**	
building	**el edificio** ◄			

cloudy	**nublado** or **nublada**	dessert	**el postre**
clown	**el payaso**	different	**diferente**
coffee	**el café**	dining room	**el comedor**
coin	**la moneda**	dinner	**la cena**
cold (flu)	**el resfriado**	dinosaur	**el dinosaurio**
		dirt	**la tierra**
		dirty	**sucio** or **sucia**
		dishes	**la vajilla**
		doctor	**el doctor**

cold (temperature)	**frío** or **fría** ▲	dog	**el perro** or **la perra** ◄
color	**el color**	doll	**la muñeca**
comb	**el peine**	dollar	**el dólar**
comet	**el cometa**	donkey	**el burro** or **la burra**
computer	**la computadora**	door	**la puerta**
cook	**el cocinero** or **la cocinera** ◄	down	**abajo**
		dragon	**el dragón**
cookies	**las galletas**	drawing	**el dibujo**
corn	**el maíz**	dress	**el vestido** ◄
corner	**la esquina**	dresser	**el tocador**
couch	**el sofá**	drinks	**las bebidas**
cough	**la tos**	drum	**el tambor**
country	**el país**	dry	**seco** or **seca**
cousin	**el primo**		
cow	**la vaca** ◄		
crayons	**los gises**		
crazy	**loco** or **loca**		
cup	**la taza**	dryer	**la secadora** ▲
curtains	**las cortinas**	duck	**el pato** or **la pata**

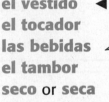

dancing	**el baile**	each	**cada**
dangerous	**peligroso** or **peligrosa**	ear	**la oreja**
dark	**oscuro** or **oscura**	early	**temprano** or **temprana**
daughter	**la hija** ◄		
day	**el día**	earrings	**los aretes**
December	**diciembre**	easy	**fácil**
deer	**el venado**	egg	**el huevo** ◄
dentist	**el** or **la dentista**	eight	**ocho**
desert	**el desierto**	eighteen	**dieciocho**
		eighty	**ochenta**
		elephant	**el elefante** or **la elefanta**
desk	**el escritorio** ▲	elevator	**el ascensor**

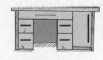

eleven	once	fifty	cincuenta
elf	el duende ◄ 	fine	bien
empty	vacío or vacía	firefighter	el bombero or
end	el fin		la bombera
engine	el motor	first	primero or
English	el inglés		primera
enough	bastante		
envelope	el sobre		
eraser	el borrador ◄		
everybody	todos or todas	fish	el pescado ▲
excellent	excelente	five	cinco
excited	emocionado or	flag	la bandera
	emocionada	floor	el piso
expensive	caro or cara	flower	la flor
eye	el ojo	fly	la mosca ◄
		folder	la carpeta
face	la cara	food	la comida
factory	la fábrica	foot	el pie
fairy	la hada	for	para
		forest	el bosque
		fork	el tenedor
		forty	cuarenta
		four	cuatro
		fourteen	catorce
fall	el otoño ▲	french fries	las papas
family	la familia		fritas ◄
fantastic	fantástico or		
	fantástica	Friday	viernes
far	lejos	friend	el amigo or la amiga
farm	la finca	from	de
fat	gordo or	fruit	la fruta
	gorda ◄	frying pan	el sartén
father	el padre	full	lleno or llena
fast	rápido or rápida	fun	la diversión ◄
faucet	el grifo	funny	chistoso or
favorite	favorito or favorita		chistosa
feather	la pluma	furniture	los muebles
February	febrero		
fence	la cerca	game	el juego
fever	la fiebre ◄	garage	el garaje
few	pocos or pocas	garden	el jardín
fifteen	quince	gas station	la gasolinera

gate	el portón	helicopter	el helicóptero ▼
ghost	el fantasma	hello	hola
giant	el gigante or	her	su
	la giganta	here	aquí
giraffe	la jirafa	highway	la carretera
girl	la niña ◄	hill	el cerro
glass	el vaso	his	su
glove	el guante	Hispanic	hispano or hispana
glue	el pegamento	homework	la tarea
God	Dios	honey	la miel
good	bueno or buena	horse	el caballo ◄
good-bye	adiós	hose	la manguera
grandfather	el abuelo	hospital	el hospital
grandmother	la abuela	hot	caliente
grape	la uva ◄	hot dog	el perro caliente
grass	el pasto	hotel	el hotel
gray	gris	hour	la hora
green	verde	house	la casa ◄
guitar	la guitarra	hug	el abrazo
		husband	el esposo

gum	el chicle ▲	I	yo
		I'm	estoy
		I'm	soy
hair	el pelo	ice	el hielo
hairbrush	el cepillo	ice cream	el helado ◄
haircut	el corte de pelo	important	importante
hallway	el pasillo	in front	enfrente
ham	el jamón	in	en
hambuger	la hamburguesa	inside	adentro
hammer	el martillo	It's	es
hand	la mano	It's	está
handkerchief	el pañuelo		
handsome	guapo ◄	jacket	la chaqueta ◄
happy	feliz	January	enero
hard	difícil	jello	la gelatina
has	tiene	joke	el chiste
he	él	juice	el jugo
he's	es	July	julio
head	la cabeza	June	junio
headache	el dolor de cabeza		
heart	el corazón		

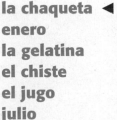

135

key	la llave	mail	el correo
king	el rey ◄	mailbox	el buzón
kiss	el beso	mail carrier	el cartero
kitchen	la cocina		or la cartera
kite	la cometa	man	el hombre ◄
kitty	el gatito or	many	muchos or
	la gatita ◄		muchas
knife	el cuchillo	map	el mapa
		March	marzo
ladder	la escalera	marker	el marcador
lady (Mrs.)	Señora (Sra.)	math	las matemáticas
lake	el lago	May	mayo
lamp	la lámpara	meat	la carne
language	el lenguaje	mechanic	el mecánico or
last	último or última		la mecánica
late	tarde ◄	medicine	la medicina
later	luego	merry-go-round	los caballitos
lazy	perezoso	milk	la leche
	or perezosa	milkshake	el batido ◄
leaf	la hoja	minute	el minuto
left	la izquierda	mirror	el espejo
leg	la pierna	Mister (Mr.)	Señor (Sr.)
lemonade	la limonada	Miss (Ms.)	Señorita (Srta.)
less	menos	Monday	lunes
lettuce	la lechuga ◄	money	el dinero
library	la biblioteca	monster	el monstruo
lights	las luces	month	el mes
lion	el león or la leona	moon	la luna
little	chico or chica	mop	el trapeador ◄
living room	la sala	more	más
long	largo or larga	morning	la mañana
love	el amor	mother	la madre
		motorcycle	la motocicleta
		mountain	la montaña
		mouse	el ratón or
			la ratona ◄
lunch	el almuerzo ▲	mouth	la boca
		movies	el cine
		mud	el lodo
magazine	la revista	music	la música
magic	la magia	my	mi

nail (body)	la uña	one	uno
nail (iron)	el clavo 	one hundred	cien
name	el nombre	one thousand	mil
napkin	la servilleta	onion	la cebolla
near	cerca	only	solamente
necessary	necesarlo or necesaria	open	abierto or abierta
		or	o
neck	el cuello	orange (color)	anaranjado or anaranjada
necklace	el collar		
neighbor	el vecino or la vecina	orange (fruit)	la naranja 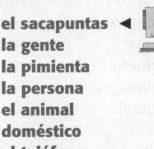
never	nunca	our	nuestro or nuestra
new	nuevo or nueva		
		outside	afuera
		overcoat	el abrigo

		page	la página
		paint	la pintura
		pajamas	el or la piyama
newspaper	el periódico ▲	pants	los pantalones ▼
nice	simpático or simpática	paper	el papel
		parents	los padres
night	la noche	park	el parque
nine	nueve	party	la fiesta
nineteen	diecinueve	pen	el lapicero
ninety	noventa	pencil	el lápiz
no one	nadie	pencil	
none	ninguno or ninguna	sharpener	el sacapuntas
nose	la nariz	people	la gente
not	no ◄	pepper	la pimienta
nothing	nada	person	la persona
November	noviembre	pet	el animal doméstico
now	ahora		
number	el número	phone	el teléfono
nurse	el enfermero or la enfermera	phone number	el número de teléfono
		photo	la foto
October	octubre	pie	el pastel
of	de	pig	el puerco or
office	la oficina		la puerca ◄
old	viejo or vieja ▲	pillow	la almohada
on	en	pilot	el or la piloto

pink	**rosado** or **rosada**			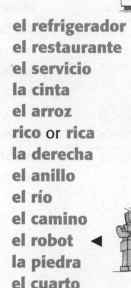
place	**el lugar**			
plane	**el avión**			
planet	**el planeta**			
plant	**la planta** ◄		refrigerator	**el refrigerador** ▲
plate	**el plato**		restaurant	**el restaurante**
playground	**el campo de recreo**		restroom	**el servicio**
please	**por favor**		ribbon	**la cinta**
pliers	**los alicates**		rice	**el arroz**
police	**la policía**		rich	**rico** or **rica**
police officer	**el** or **la**		right	**la derecha**
	policía ◄		ring	**el anillo**
pool	**la piscina**		river	**el río**
poor	**pobre**		road	**el camino**
popcorn	**las palomitas**		robot	**el robot** ◄	
possible	**posible**		rock	**la piedra**
post office	**la oficina de correo**		room	**el cuarto**
pot	**la olla**			
potato	**la papa**		sad	**triste**
present	**el regalo**		salad	**la ensalada**
pretty	**bonito** or			
	bonita ◄			
prince	**el príncipe**			
princess	**la princesa**			
proud	**orgulloso** or			
	orgullosa			
puppy	**el perrito** or			
	la perrita		salesperson	**el vendedor** or
purple	**morado** or **morada**			**la vendedora** ▲
purse	**la bolsa**		salt	**la sal**
puzzle	**el rompecabezas**		same	**mismo** or **misma**
			sandwich	**el emparedado**
			Saturday	**sábado**
queen	**la reina** ◄		saucer	**el platillo**
			sausage	**la salchicha**
rabbit	**el conejo** or		saw	**el serrucho** ▼
	la coneja		scarf	**la bufanda**
radio	**el** or **la radio**		school	**la escuela**
rain	**la lluvia**		science	**la ciencia**	
raincoat	**el impermeable**		scissors	**las tijeras**
rake	**el rastrillo**		screwdriver	**el atornillador**
reading	**la lectura**		sea	**el mar**
red	**rojo** or **roja**			

second	el segundo	smile	la sonrisa
secretary	el secretario or	snail	el caracol 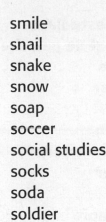
	la secretaria	snake	la culebra
		snow	la nieve
		soap	el jabón
		soccer	el fútbol
		social studies	los estudios sociales
		socks	los calcetines
seesaw	el subibaja ▲	soda	el refresco ◄
September	septiembre	soldier	el or la soldado
seven	siete	some	algunos or
seventeen	diecisiete		algunas
seventy	setenta	someone	alguien
shampoo	el champú	something	algo
she	ella	sometimes	a veces
she's	es	son	el hijo
sheep	la oveja	song	la canción
sheet	la sábana	soon	pronto
shirt	la camisa ◄	soup	la sopa ◄
shoes	los zapatos	space	el espacio
short	bajo or baja	spaceship	la nave espacial
shorts	los pantalones cortos	Spanish	el español
shoulder	el hombro	special	especial
shovel	la pala ◄	spider	la araña
shower	la ducha	sponge	la esponja ◄
side	el lado	spoon	la cuchara
sidewalk	la acera	sports	los deportes
sign	el letrero	spring	la primavera
sink	el lavabo ◄	stairs	las escaleras
sister	la hermana	star	la estrella
six	seis	state	el estado
sixteen	dieciséis	steak	el bistec ◄
sixty	sesenta	stereo	el estéreo
size	el tamaño	stomach	el estómago
skateboard	la patineta	stomachache	el dolor de estómago
skates	los patines	store	la tienda
skirt	la falda ◄	story	el cuento
slide	el resbalador	stove	la estufa
slippers	las pantuflas	strawberry	la fresa ◄
slow	lento or lenta	street	la calle
smart	inteligente	strong	fuerte

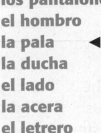

student	el or la estudiante	they're	son
stuffed animal	el animal de peluche	thin	delgado or
subway	el metro		delgada ◄
sugar	el azúcar	thing	la cosa
suit	el traje	third	tercero or
Sunday	domingo		tercera
supermarket	el supermercado	thirteen	trece
sweater	el suéter	thirty	treinta
sweet	dulce	this	esto or esta
swing	el columpio ◄	those	esos or esas
		throat	la garganta
table	la mesa	three	tres ◄
tall	alto or alta	Thursday	jueves
tea	el té	tie	la corbata
		tiger	el tigre
		time	el tiempo
		tired	cansado or cansada
		to the	al
		to	a
		today	hoy
teacher	el maestro or	together	juntos or juntas
	la maestra ▲	toilet	el excusado
team	el equipo	tomato	el tomate ◄
teddy bear	el osito or la osita	tomorrow	mañana
teeth	los dientes	tool	la herramienta
telephone	el teléfono	toothache	el dolor de muela
		toothbrush	el cepillo de dientes
		toothpaste	la pasta de dientes
		towel	la toalla ◄
		town	el pueblo
		toy	el juguete
television	el televisor ▲	traffic light	el semáforo
ten	diez	train	el tren
thanks	gracias	trashcan	el bote de basura
that	eso or esa	tree	el árbol
the	el, la, los, or las	tricks	los trucos
their	su		
then	entonces		
there	allí		
thermometer	el termómetro ◄		
these	estos or estas	truck	el camión ▲
they're	están	T-shirt	la camiseta

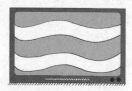

Tuesday	martes	window	la ventana ◄
turkey	el pavo	winter	el invierno
turtle	la tortuga	witch	la bruja
twelve	doce	with	con
twenty	veinte	without	sin
two	dos ◄	wizard	el mago ◄
		woman	la mujer
ugly	feo or fea	word	la palabra
under	abajo	work	el trabajo
underwear	la ropa interior	worker	el trabajador or
United States	los Estados Unidos		la trabajadora
up	arriba	world	el mundo
vacations	las vacaciones	yard	el patio
vacuum cleaner	la aspiradora	year	el año
		yellow	amarillo or amarilla
		yes	sí
		yesterday	ayer
vegetables	los vegetales ▲		
very	muy		
vitamin	la vitamina		
waiter	el mesero or		
	la mesera		
wall	la pared	you (formal)	usted ▲
wallet	la cartera	you guys	ustedes
washer	la lavadora	you (informal)	tú
watch	el reloj	you're	eres
water	el agua ◄	you're	estás
watermelon	la sandía	young person	el muchacho
we	nosotros or nosotras		or la
weak	débil		muchacha ◄
weather	el tiempo	young	joven
Wednesday	miércoles	your	tu
week	la semana		
white	blanco or blanca	zero	cero
wife	la esposa	zoo	el zoológico

More Fun Things to Say in SPANISH

And you?	¿Y tú?
Bless you!	¡Salud!
Can I help you?	¿Cómo puedo ayudarte?
Congratulations!	¡Felicitaciones!
Do you understand?	¿Entiendes?
Excuse me.	Con permiso.
Get well!	¡Que se mejore!
Go ahead.	Pase.
Good afternoon.	Buenas tardes.
Good idea!	¡Buena idea!
Good luck!	¡Buena suerte!
Good morning.	Buenos días.
Good night.	Buenas noches.
Good-bye.	Adiós.
Happy birthday!	¡Feliz cumpleaños!
Happy Easter!	¡Felices Pascuas!
Happy holidays!	¡Felices fiestas!
Happy New Year!	¡Próspero año nuevo!
Have a good time!	¡Que disfrute!
Have a nice day!	¡Que tenga buen día!
Have a nice trip!	¡Buen viaje!
Hello or Hi.	Hola.
Help!	¡Socorro!
How are you?	¿Cómo estás?
How do you say it?	¿Cómo se dice?
How do you spell it?	¿Cómo se deletrea?
How old are you?	¿Cuántos años tienes?
How sad!	¡Qué triste!
How's it going!	¡Qué tal!
I agree!	¡De acuerdo!
I don't know.	No sé.
I don't understand.	No entiendo.
I hope so!	¡Ojalá!
I remember!	¡Yo recuerdo!
I speak a little.	Hablo un poquito.
I'm hungry.	Tengo hambre.
I'm learning Spanish.	Estoy aprendiendo español.
I'm so glad!	¡Me alegro!
I'm sorry.	Lo siento.

Isn't that right?	¿No es cierto?
Let's go!	¡Vamos!
May I come in?	¿Se puede?
Maybe!	¡Quizás!
Me, neither!	¡Yo tampoco!
Me, too!	¡Yo también!
Merry Christmas!	¡Feliz Navidad!
My name is . . .	Me llamo . . .
Nice to meet you!	¡Mucho gusto!
No problem!	¡Ningún problema!
No wonder!	¡Con razón!
Nothing much!	¡Sin novedad!
Of course!	¡Por supuesto!
Pardon me.	Perdón.
Please.	Por favor.
Ready?	¿Listos?
Really?	¿Es verdad?
Same to you.	Igualmente.
See you later.	Hasta luego.
So what!	¡Qué importa!
Sort of.	Más o menos.
Sure!	¡Claro!
Thanks a lot.	Muchas gracias.
That's OK!	¡Está bien!
I think so!	¡Creo que sí!
That's too bad!	¡Qué lástima!
Very well.	Muy bien.
Welcome!	¡Bienvenidos!
What does it mean?	¿Qué significa?
What happened?	¿Qué pasó?
What time is it?	¿Qué hora es?
What's happening?	¿Qué pasa?
What's your name?	¿Cómo te llamas?
Who's calling?	¿Quién habla?
Why not!	¡Cómo no!
Wow!	¡Caramba!
Yes	Sí
You're welcome.	De nada.

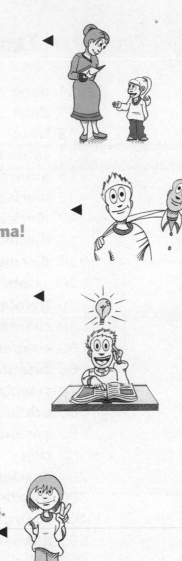

Los Números

0 cero	11 once	
1 uno	12 doce	
	13 trece	
	14 catorce	
2 dos	15 quince	
	16 dieciséis	
	17 diecisiete	
3 tres	18 dieciocho	
	19 diecinueve	
	20 veinte	
4 cuatro	30 treinta	
	40 cuarenta	
	50 cincuenta	
5 cinco	60 sesenta	
	70 setenta	
	80 ochenta	
6 seis	90 noventa	
	100 cien	
	200 doscientos	
7 siete	300 trescientos	
	400 cuatrocientos	
	500 quinientos	
8 ocho	600 seiscientos	
	700 setecientos	
	800 ochocientos	
9 nueve	900 novecientos	
	1000 mil	
	1156 mil ciento cincuenta y seis	
10 diez	10000 diez mil	
	100000 cien mil	
	1000000 un millón	

ACTION-WORD FLASHCARDS

These are called VERB INFINITIVES. If you learn these, you can really speak a lot of Spanish!

Cut out each one carefully, and keep them all together with a rubber band. Put them in a safe place, so you can take them out whenever you want to practice. Why don't you start today?

to ask

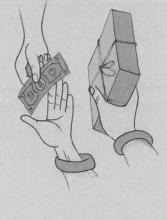

to buy

to arrive

to burn

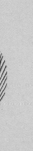

to answer

to brush
one's hair

comprar

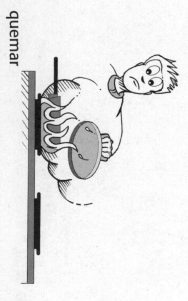

preguntar

quemar

llegar

cepillarse

contestar

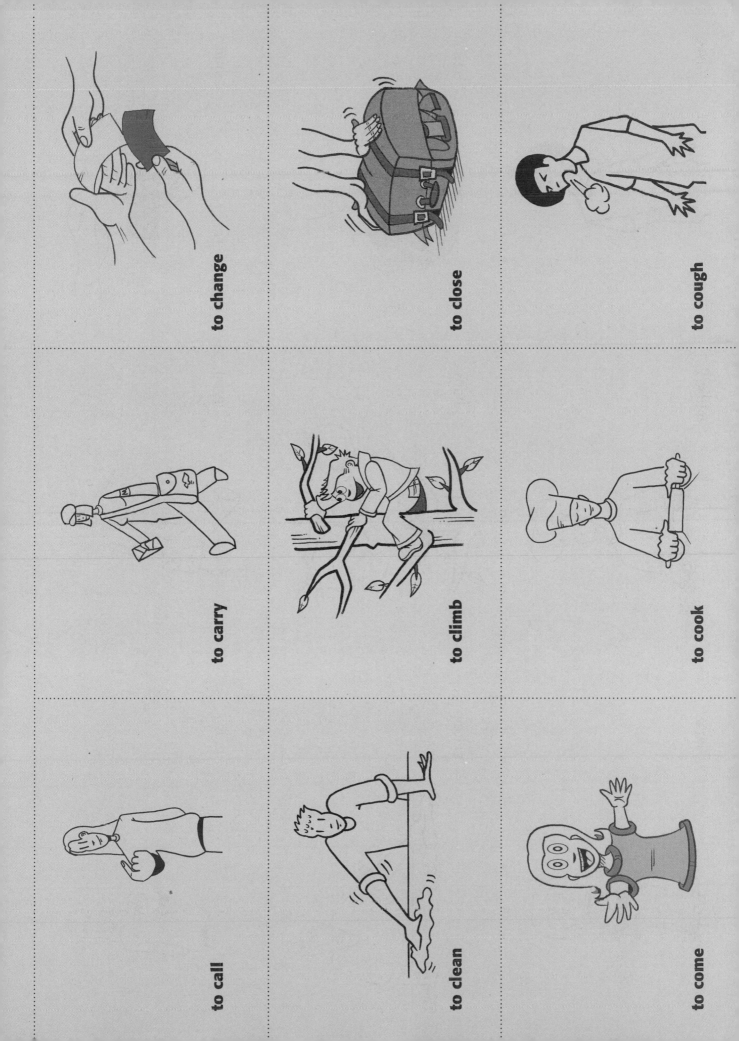

to change

to close

to cough

to carry

to climb

to cook

to call

to clean

to come

toser

cerrar

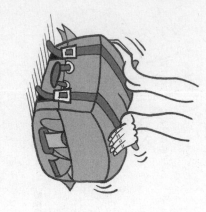

cambiar

cocinar

subir

llevar

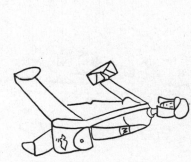

venir

limpiar

llamar

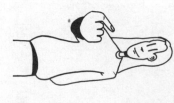

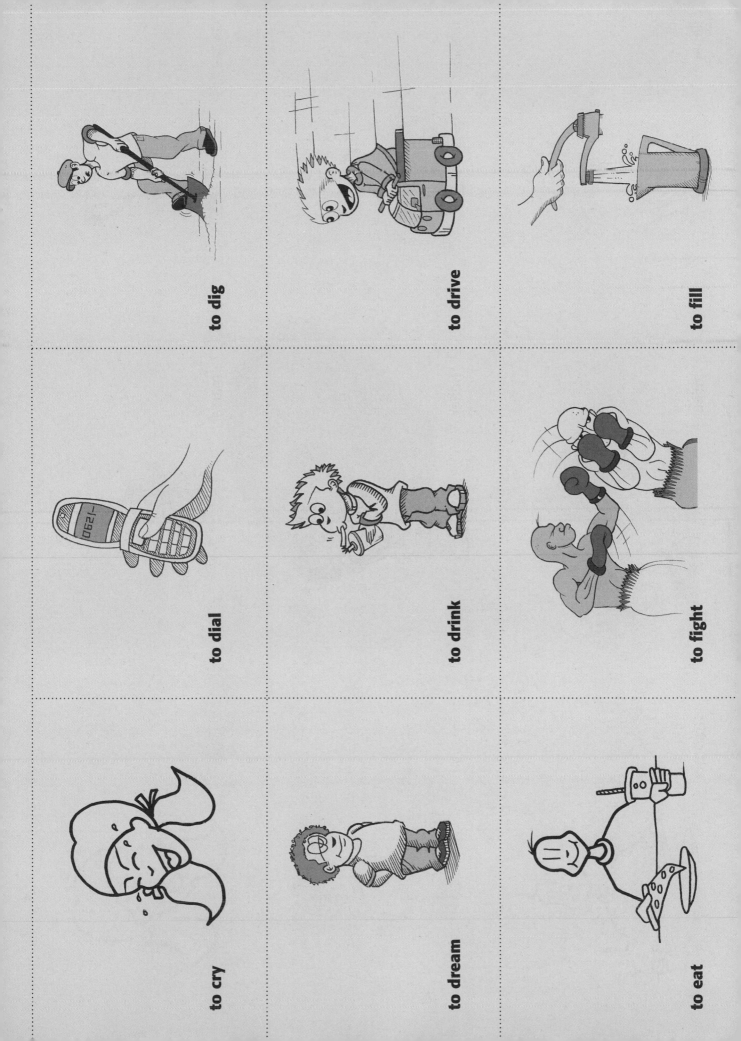

to dig

to drive

to fill

to dial

to drink

to fight

to cry

to dream

to eat

llenar

manejar

cavar

pelear

beber

marcar

comer

soñar

llorar

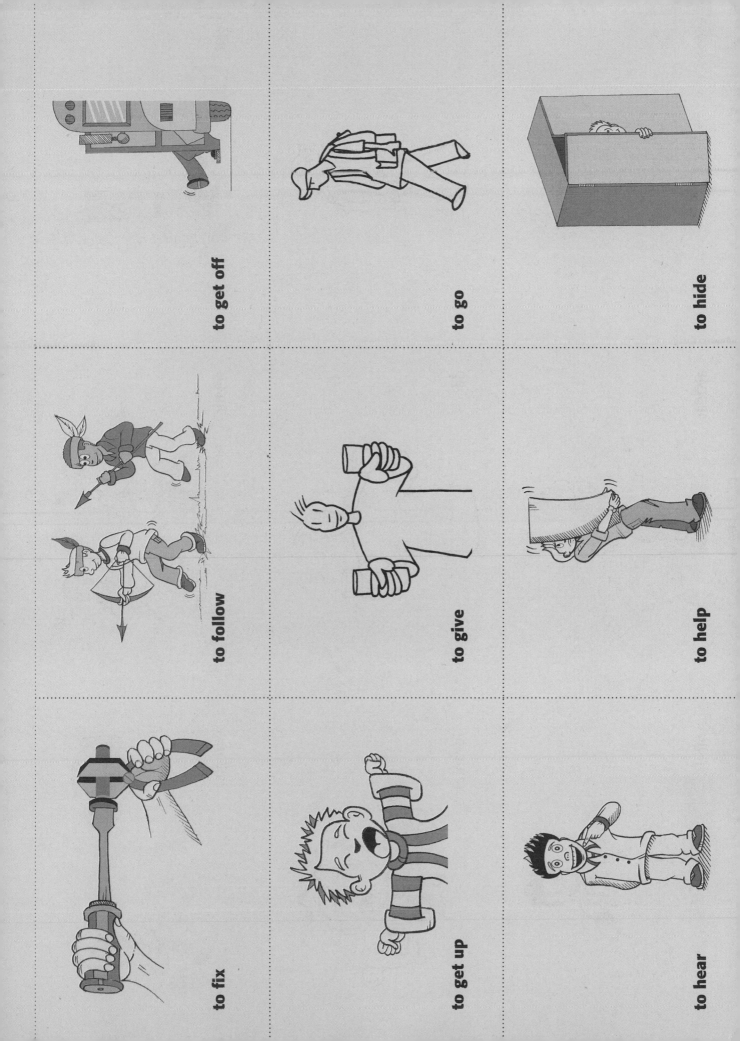

to get off

to go

to hide

to follow

to give

to help

to fix

to get up

to hear

esconder

ir

bajar

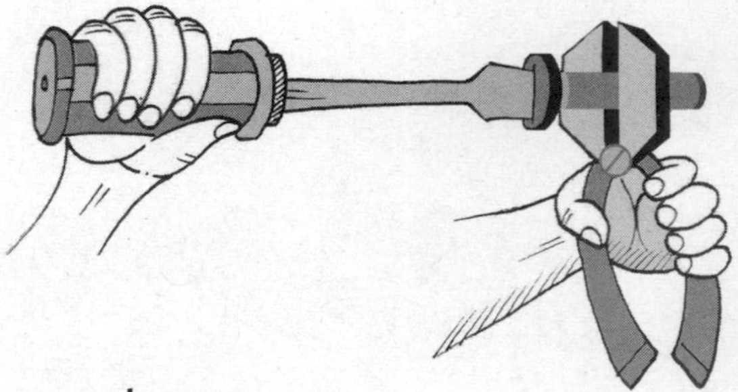

ayudar

dar

seguir

oír

levantarse

arreglar

to jump

to leave

to listen

to hug

to learn

to lift

to hit

to kiss

to lie down

escuchar

salir

saltar

levantar

aprender

abrazar

acostarse

besar

pegar

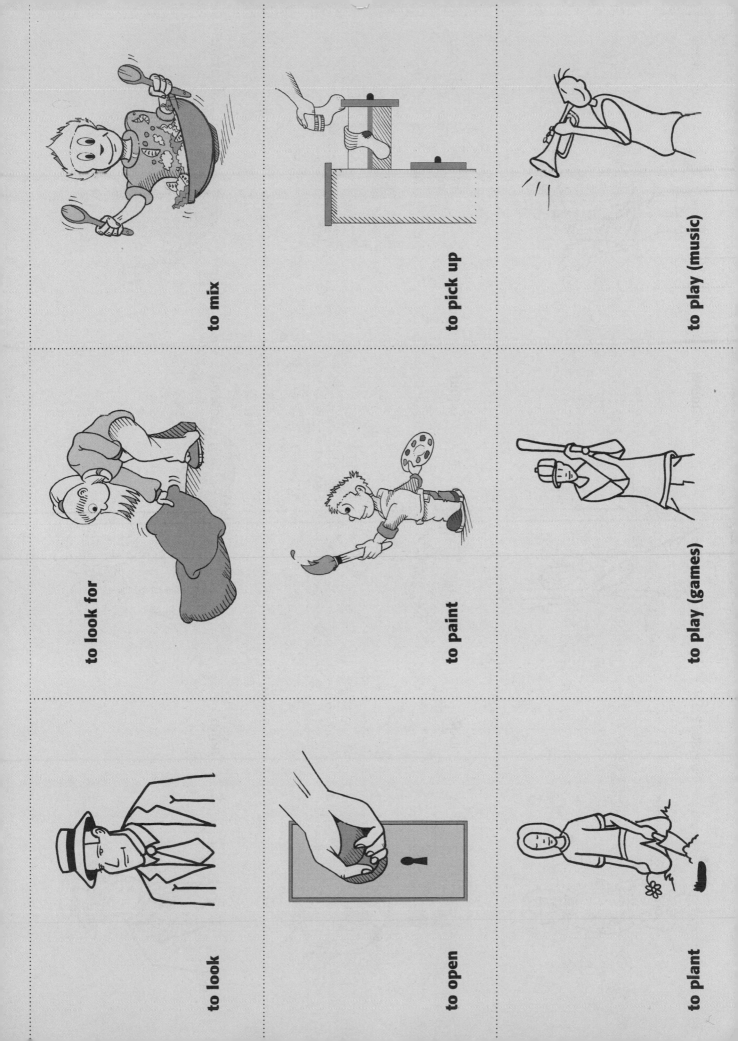

to mix

to pick up

to play (music)

to look for

to paint

to play (games)

to look

to open

to plant

tocar

recoger

mezclar

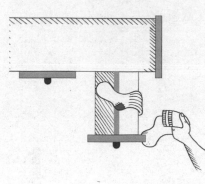

jugar

pintar

buscar

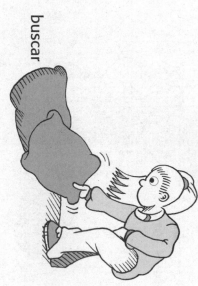

plantar

abrir

mirar

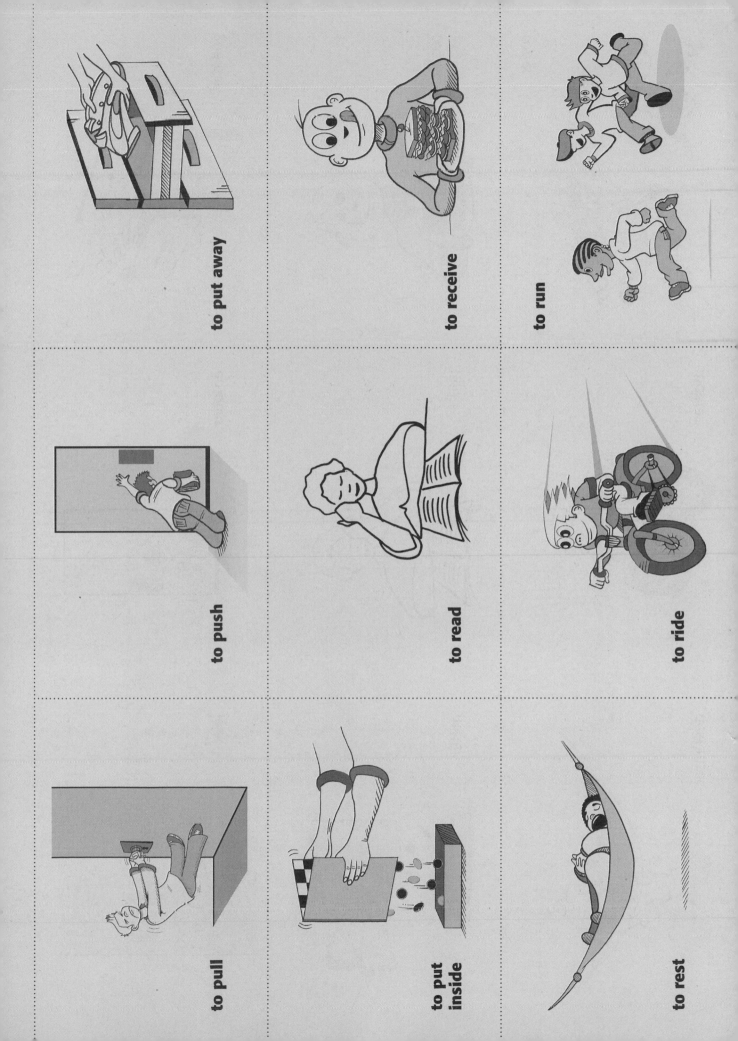

to put away

to receive

to run

to push

to read

to ride

to pull

to put inside

to rest

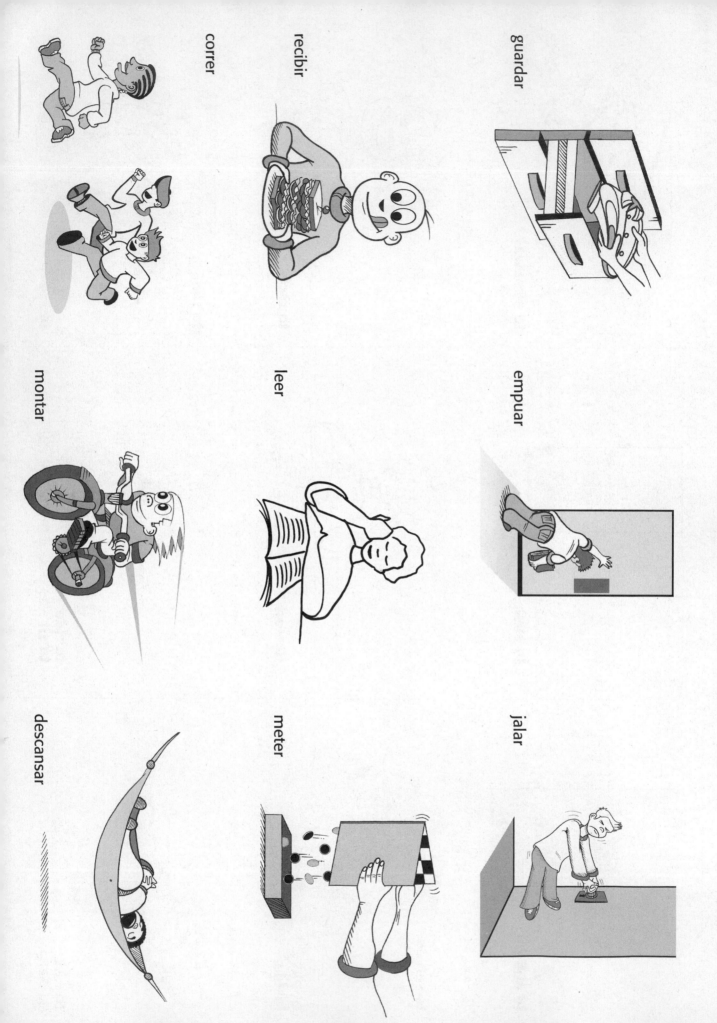

correr

recibir

guardar

montar

leer

empuar

descansar

meter

jalar

to send

to show

to speak

to sell

to shave oneself

to sit down

to scream

to serve

to sleep

mandar

mostrar

hablar

vender

afeitarse

sentarse

gritar

servir

dormir

to throw

to turn off

to wake up

to sweep

to travel

to wait

to study

to touch

to turn on

tirar

apagar

despertar

viajar

barrer

prender

tocar

estudiar

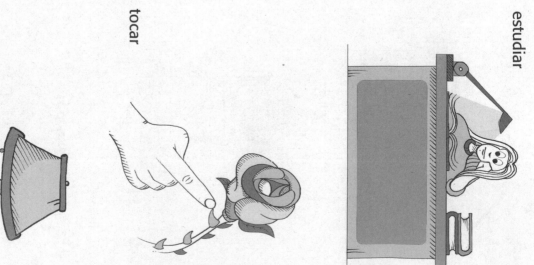

to wash

to water

to yawn

to want

to watch TV

to write

to walk

to wash oneself

to work

lavar

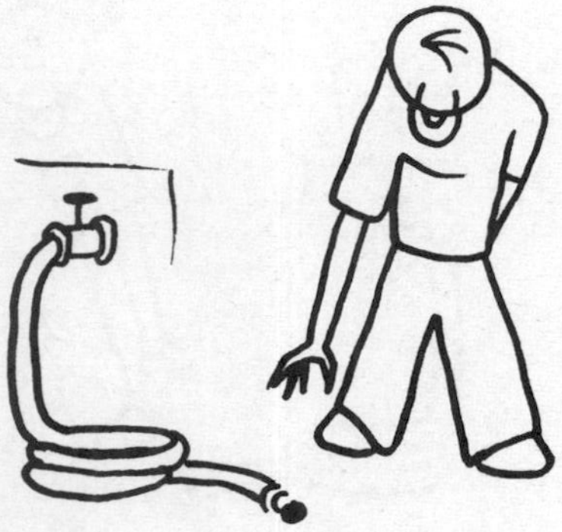

regar

bostezar

querer

mirar televisión

escribir

caminar

lavarse

trabajar